A–Z

OF

WEYMOUTH AND PORTLAND

PLACES - PEOPLE - HISTORY

Michael Burgess

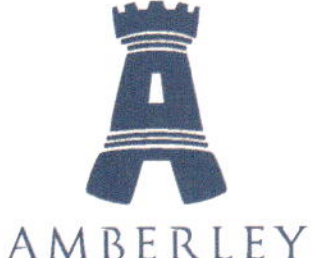

AMBERLEY

First published 2026

Amberley Publishing
The Hill, Stroud, Gloucestershire, GL5 4EP
www.amberley-books.com

Copyright © Michael Burgess, 2026

The right of Michael Burgess to be identified
as the Author of this work has been asserted in
accordance with the Copyrights, Designs and
Patents Act 1988.

ISBN 978 1 3981 2369 4 (print)
ISBN 978 1 3981 2370 0 (ebook)

British Library Cataloguing in Publication Data.
A catalogue record for this book is available
from the British Library.

Origination by Amberley Publishing.
Printed in Great Britain.

Appointed GPSR EU Representative: Easy
Access System Europe Oü, 16879218
Address: Mustamäe tee 50, 10621, Tallinn, Estonia
Contact Details: gpsr.requests@easproject.com,
+358 40 500 3575

Contents

Introduction

Weymouth is a world-famous holiday resort that can trace it's history back to Roman times. It saw the introduction of the Black Death to England, times of battle during the English Civil War, and was the starting point for thousands of American soldiers bound for the D-Day landings and the Normandy campaign that followed during the Second World War.

Famous author Thomas Hardy used it as the template for the town of Budmouth in his novel *Far from the Madding Crowd*, and others.

The visits of King George III brought fame to the town, and a dedicated Royalist following saw a statue erected to him for his Golden Jubilee, and others erected to Queen Victoria for hers.

Today Weymouth is a bustling tourist resort served by mainline railways, road-based public transport services and, especially following the improvements to the roads carried out to coincide with the 2012 Olympics, easy access for private motorists. But look beyond the brightness of the modern tourist industries and you will soon find signs of Weymouth's earlier history and many fascinating modern facts. Some of them you will find described in this book. I hope you enjoy it and that it makes the time you spend in Weymouth all the more entertaining.

As ever with a book of this size there are limits to what can be covered, so I apologise in advance if I have missed mentioning any of your favourite places.

Air Sea Rescue

If you look down from Portland towards Chesil beach you will see in the foreground a large white hangar and a helicopter landing pad. Up until 30 June 2017 this was the location of a Coastguard Search and Rescue helicopter organised by the Coastguard.

This was initially the home of an air sea rescue service carried out by the Royal Naval Air Service under the title of HMS Osprey (all Royal Navy land bases are referred to as HMS as if they were seagoing vessels) from 1959, the operations being carried out by a range of squadrons.

In 1999 the Portland Search and Rescue base, now renamed Osprey Quay, was listed as the second busiest the UK with no fewer than 270 callouts that year. In the same year the RNAS base was closed and the area passed into private hands.

From 1 July 2017 the airbase was taken over by Heli operations who offer search and rescue training to operators around the world and maintain a rest and refuelling capacity at the site for search and rescue helicopters working in the Weymouth area.

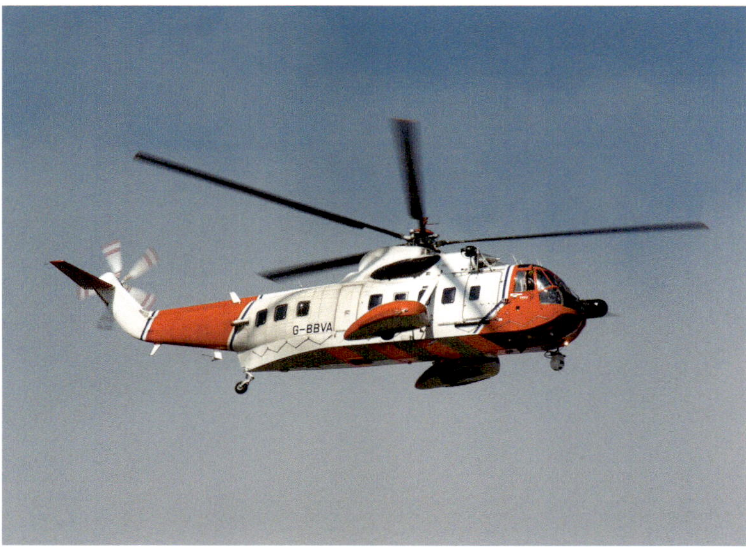

A Sikorsky S-61N Coastguard air sea rescue helicopter.

ANZAC Memorial

At the northern end of the Esplanade you will find a three-sided obelisk of Portland stone atop a plinth of the same material. Carved into the surface of the plinth you will find two sets of hats, one a classic Australian bush hat with the traditional upturned right-hand brim atop a British pattern steel helmet while on the other side you will find a New Zealand-style soft hat atop another helmet.

Sculpted by John Sellman, the monument is to the thousands of wounded ANZAC (Australian and New Zealand Army Corps) and NZEF (New Zealand Expeditionary Force) volunteer soldiers who passed through the camps and hospitals of Weymouth and their dedicated hospital facility in the Verne Citadel on Portland during the First World War.

The monument was unveiled on 1 June 2005 by Reverend Eric Mitchell, ninety years after the first wounded Australian and New Zealand soldiers arrived in Dorset during the ill-fated Gallipoli campaign of 1915. Later, others followed them from the battlefields of the Western Front and the Middle East. No fewer than ninety ANZAC soldiers died in Weymouth and lie buried in war graves in the area.

The memorial is located opposite the Hotel Prince Regent which was at that time known as Burdon's military hospital. The legend at the base of the landward face says it all: 'They came from afar in the cause of freedom.'

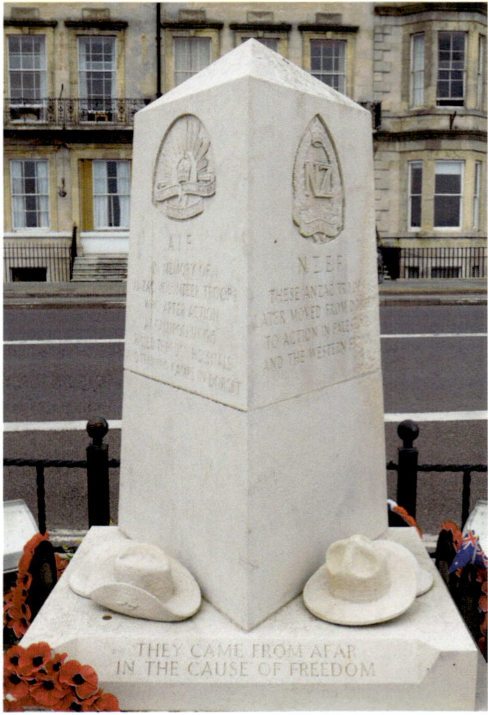

The memorial to ANZAC soldiers sits at the northern end of the Esplanade.

Every year a wreath-laying ceremony is held at the memorial on 25 April at 11.00 a.m., where wreaths are laid by veterans and local dignitaries, often with some from as far afield as Australia and New Zealand themselves. This marks the date of the first day of the landings at Gallipoli, the ANZAC's first major involvement in the First World War.

A steel plaque on the outside of the Hotel Prince Regent opposite the monument also marks the passage of these brave soldiers. It was unveiled in 2015 on the 100th anniversary of Gallipoli.

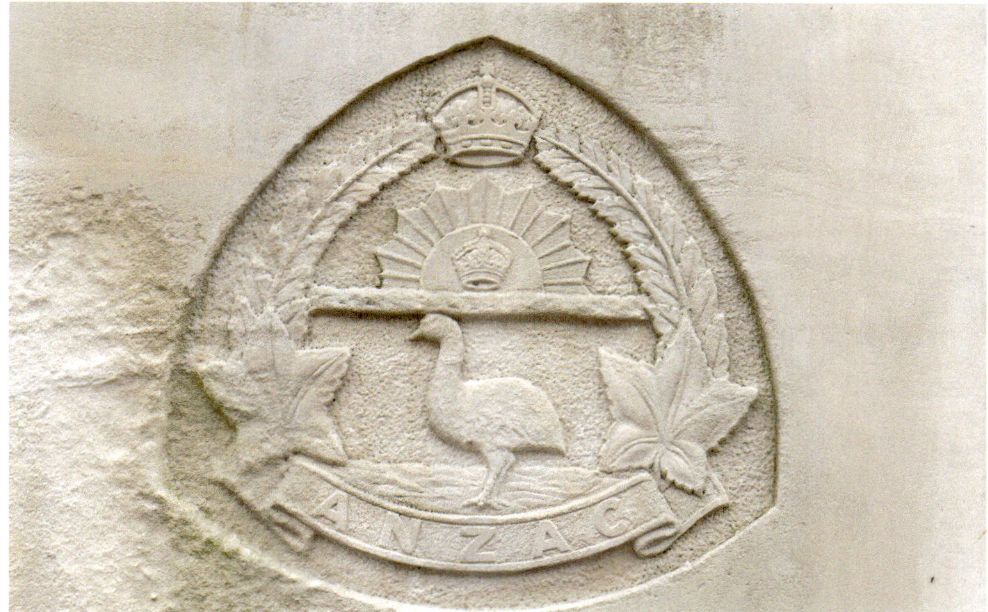

Above: The ANZAC badge is proudly displayed on the landward side of the monument.

Right: This ANZAC memorial plaque is displayed on the Hotel Prince Regent opposite the monument.

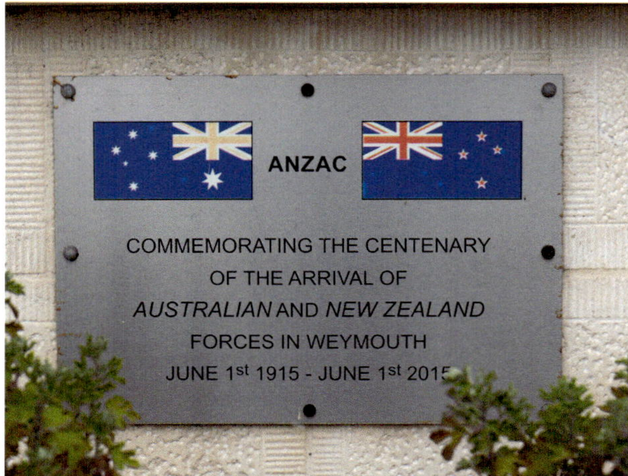

Bathing Machine

Sitting in front of the statue of King George III is a strange-looking contraption that looks for all the world like a garden shed on wheels. This is a recreation of something that appeared at the very dawn of the seaside holiday, a bathing machine – essentially a form of mobile changing room that enabled modest visitors to Weymouth to change into their brief (for the time) bathing costumes and be pulled down to the edge of the water. From their machine they could then disembark directly into the water away from prying and curious eyes.

The concept originated in Scarborough, North Yorkshire, which lays claim to being the first seaside resort as we understand the term today. The bathing machine was

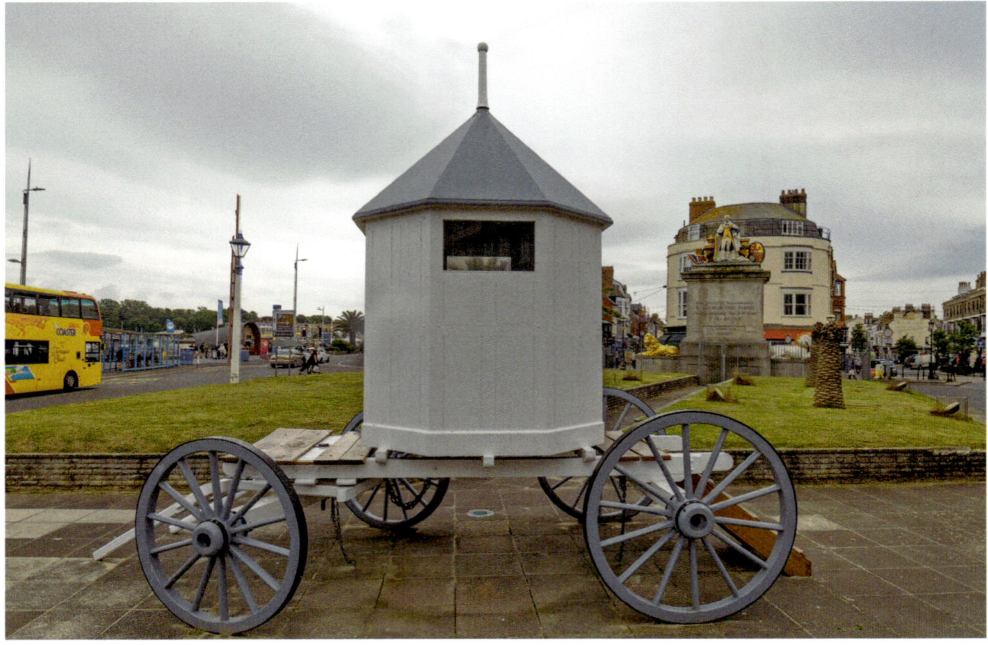

The bathing machine replica sits by the King's statue at the southern end of the Esplanade.

described in an early text as 'a curious contrivance of wooden houses moveable on wheels'. There are photographs from the Georgian and Victorian periods showing whole lines of bathing machines lined up at the water's edge at popular resorts.

The fashion for salt-water bathing arose during the eighteenth century when doctors recommended it as a cure for a whole range of conditions. Medical advice such as this led to the first of many visits to Weymouth by King George III in 1789. He would visit Weymouth every year from 1791 to 1802 to take the salt-water therapy his physicians recommended.

According to legend, when King George first stepped out of his bathing machine into the water on 7 July 1791 a band emerged from an adjoining bathing machine and played 'God Save the King'. His Royal Highness was helped into and out of the waters by two ladies who gloried in the official title of 'Royal Dippers' and who wore bathing costumes embroidered with the legend 'God Save the King' about their waists. The King himself, according to reports of the time, preferred to follow the fashion for men to bathe unclothed.

Later visits passed with less fanfare and he had created a personal bathing machine that was octagonal in shape and featured the royal coat of arms above the door. The bathing machine here is a replica of that machine. It was installed at this location in 2012 in time for the Golden Jubilee of Queen Elizabeth II.

From 1810, long after the King had ceased to visit, local by-laws required all bathers to use bathing machines to approach the water, and visitors were required to pay more for their use than local residents.

As late as 1934 the Weymouth bathing saloon company was still running nearly forty bathing machines on Weymouth beach.

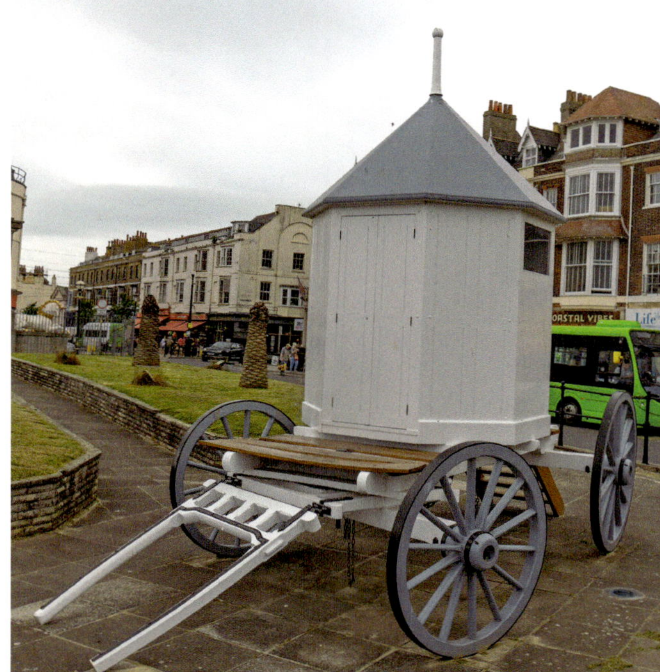

The machine was pulled to the water's edge by horse to allow modesty to the bather.

Beach

Weymouth's beach has been the main draw to the holidaying public since King George III started his patronage, and much later when the railway arrived.

It is a long, sweeping beach in a long gently curving arc with the golden sand sloping slightly out into the sea (which made it ideal for early bathers who wished to approach the water in complete modesty using bathing machines). The central or resort beach in the middle of Weymouth Bay and overlooked by the splendid Georgian town is of soft sand, while the quieter beaches at either end at Greenhill and Preston are of shingle.

Over the years Weymouth beach has won many awards, including many Blue Flags for general quality, and is recognised as one of the UK's top beaches by the Marine Conservation Society. In 2024 Weymouth beach was awarded first place in the UK (it had come second in 2023) and nineteenth place in the whole of Europe in the Tripadvisor Travellers' Choice Awards for best beach. Also in 2023 it was voted best beach in the UK by readers of the *Times* and *Sunday Times* newspapers.

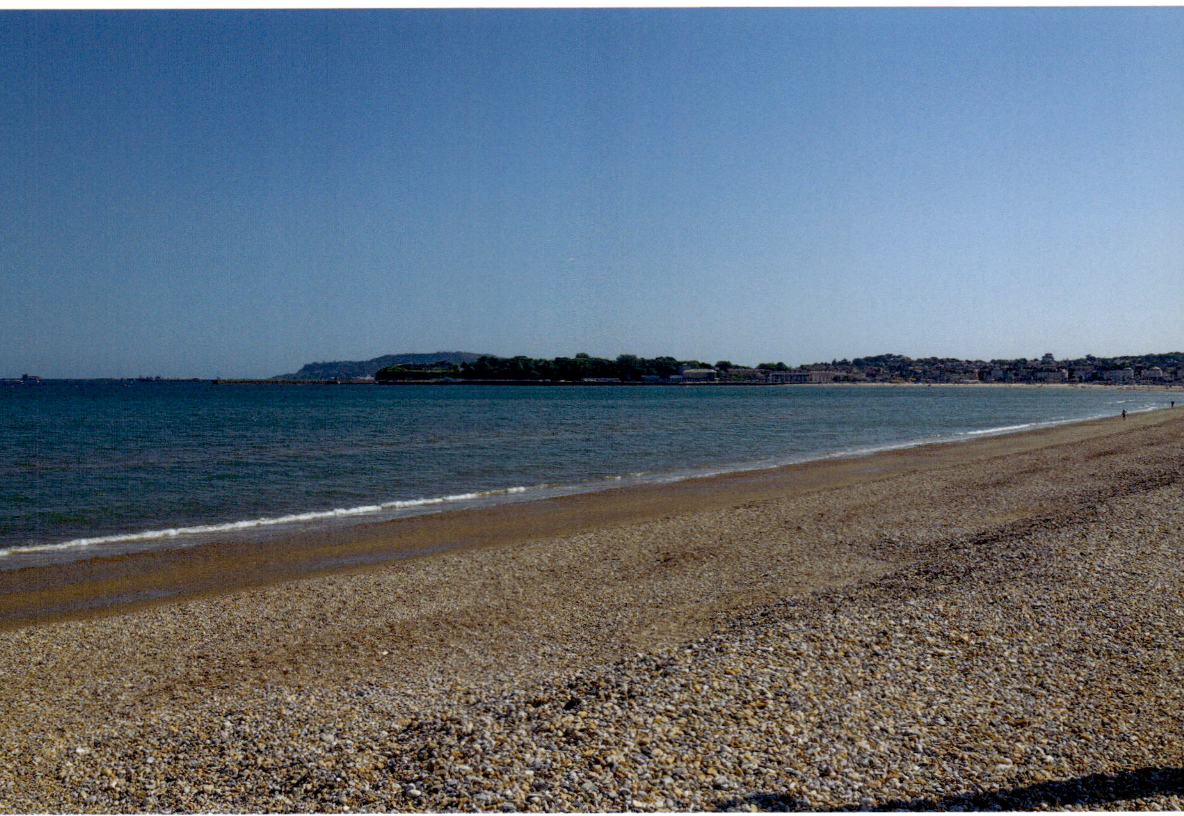

The famed sweeping arc of Weymouth beach.

Bee Orchid

The particular conditions on Portland make it a haven for the rare bee orchid and all through June and July, if you keep a careful eye at knee level, you may be lucky enough to see them in full bloom. Growing best in dry chalk and limestone grassland, the area around the Tout Quarry Sculpture Park and Nature Reserve is a particularly fruitful hunting area as it is not as disturbed by passing human and animal traffic as many other areas are.

The bee orchid was once common in southern England (it is the county flower of Bedfordshire), but pressures of the environment and human habitation has made it far rarer than it once was. A cunning plant, the flower in bloom resembles the figure of a female bee at the flower drinking nectar. The male bee, on seeing the female engrossed, attempts to mount energetically and the resulting movements pollinate the flower.

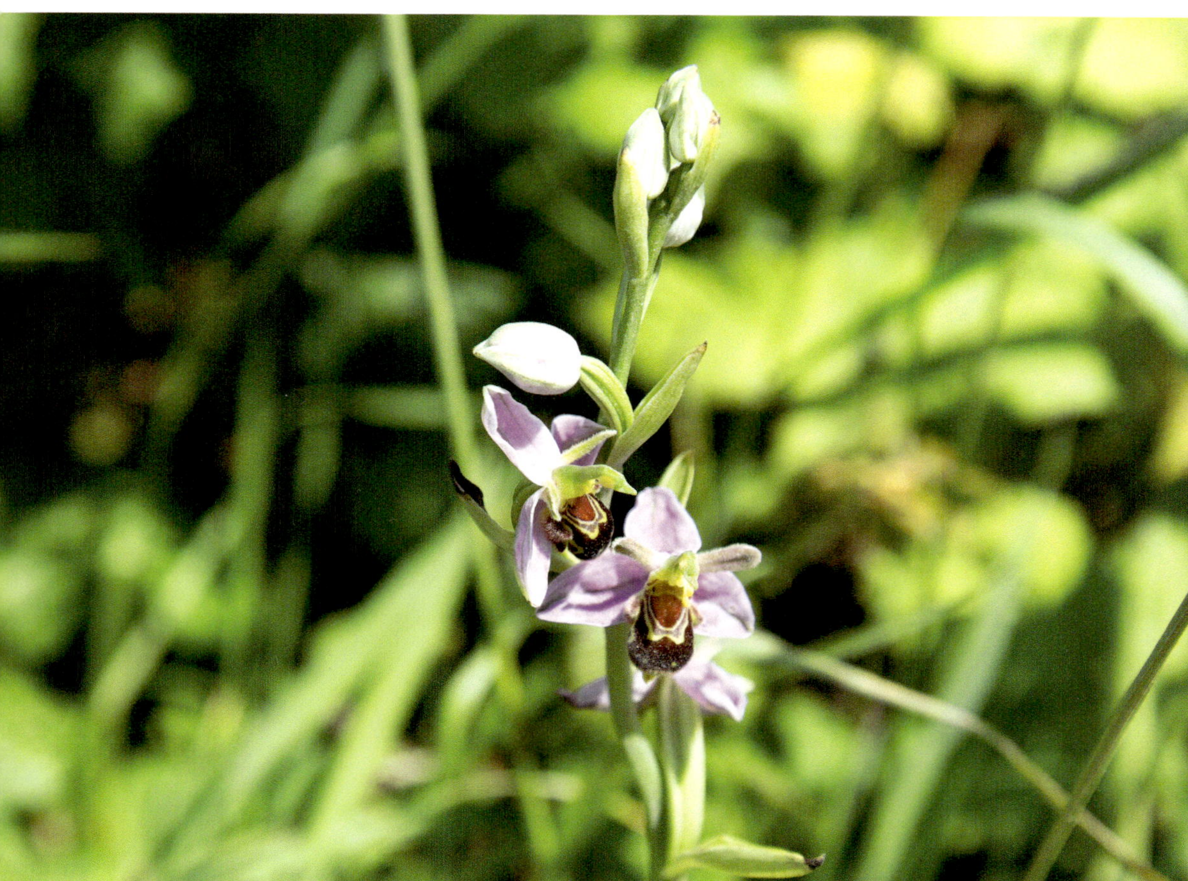

The bee orchid grows widely in the conditions found on Portland.

Black Dog Public House

The Black Dog public house claims to be the oldest hostelry in the town and is one of the few Saxon-frame buildings still in use in England. A date of 1621 is shown on the wall of the current public house but the rear of the building has been proved to be far older. The smaller stature of the building makes it stand out alongside the large nineteenth-century buildings that flank it, and later buildings now surround the stone-paved courtyard at the rear. Unusually, the floor level of the pub is lower than that of the street and patrons step down into the interior.

The Black Dog was originally known as The Dove when it was built during the reign of Queen Elizabeth I and retained that name until a contract was established in Weymouth for trade with the new territories of Newfoundland and Labrador.

The landlord of The Dove purchased what was reputed to be the first black Newfoundland Labrador dog in the UK. People travelled for miles around to see this unique dog and the landlord changed the name of his establishment to celebrate the animal that was bringing him so much extra trade.

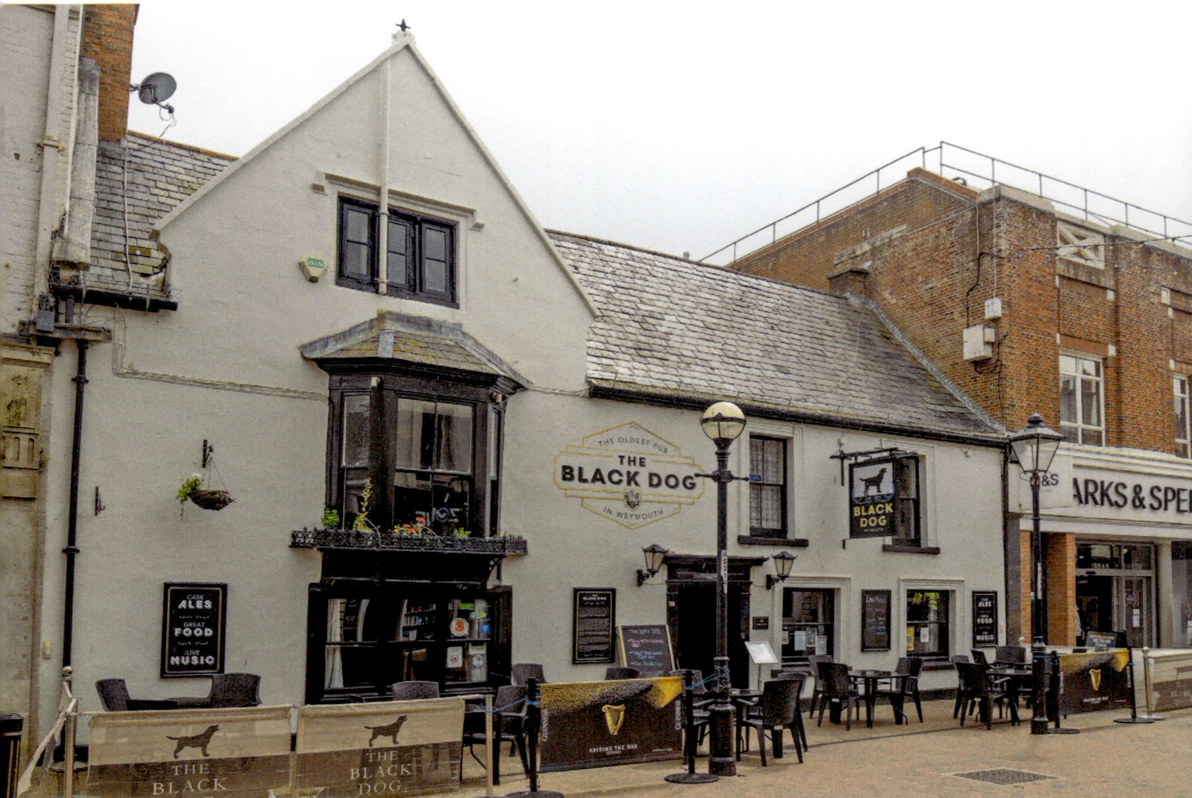

The Black Dog public house on St Mary Street.

The pub is famous and much publicised for being the scene of two murders. During the Battle of Weymouth during the English Civil War merchant William Courtney from Taunton Dene in Somerset was murdered by the landlord John Chiles to steal the £288 in gold and £12 in silver he was carrying. The body was dumped into the harbour water, no doubt in the hope that another body would not be noticed while a battle raged around them.

Sadly for Chiles the body was recognised and he was arrested, and the murder linked to him through the testimony of his wife.

The second murder took place in 1758 when a smuggler by the name of Richard Hawkins was whipped to death in the fireplace.

On a happier note, writer Daniel Defoe was inspired to write his famous book *Robinson Crusoe* after visiting Weymouth and meeting a formerly shipwrecked mariner by the name of Alexander Selkirk in the Black Dog pub.

1804 saw the visiting King George III patronising the Black Dog with the German Legion troops assigned to guard his person.

The Black Dog was given listed building status in June 1970.

Budmouth

Author Thomas Hardy famously created a whole fictional world for his 'Wessex' novels, much of it using Dorset and the adjoining parts of other counties as a template. Nearby Dorchester became Casterbridge, and Weymouth became Budmouth.

Today the name lives on in real life in the form of Budmouth Academy (formerly Budmouth College) in Weymouth and the Budmouth Community Sports Centre on Portland.

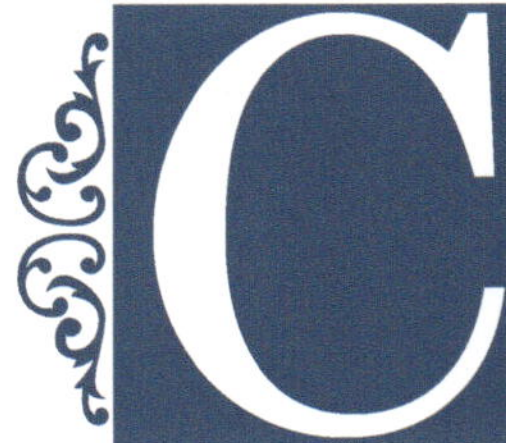

Cannonball

If you walk along Maiden Street today you will find a set of small but usually scrupulously clean public toilets, a branch of the RAFA (RAF Association) and a whole range of pubs and hospitality venues. But look up above the entrance to the ladies' toilets and you will see something unusual. A cannonball is lodged in the wall which dates from Weymouth's brief but bloody involvement in the English Civil War. Opinions and legends differ as to its exact origin, some saying it was fired from a Royalist shop in the harbour, others that it was fired from Nothe Fort, but it became embedded in what was then the local headquarters building of Royal Naval Patrol.

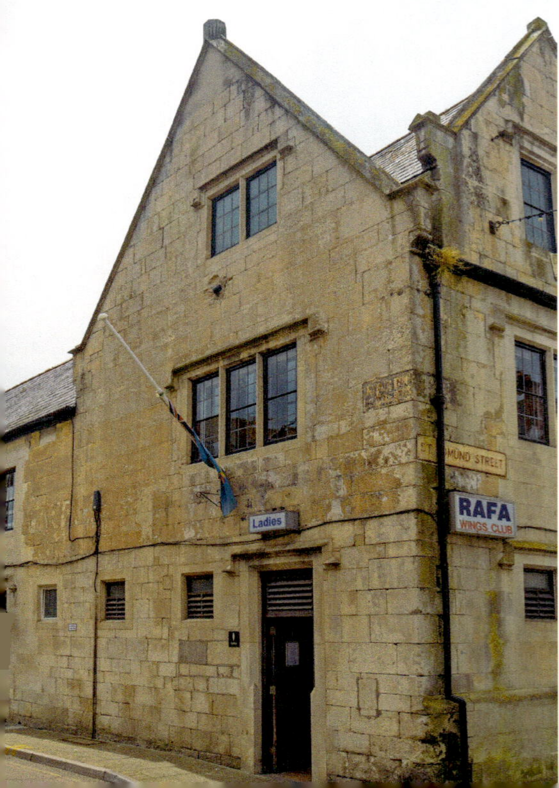

Look up in Maiden Street and you will be rewarded with the sight of a cannonball in the wall.

The conflicts in and around Weymouth occurred in February 1645 and became known as the Crabchurch Conspiracy which intended to place the important port of Weymouth under Royalist control.

Weymouth and Melcombe Regis were under the control of a foot regiment of Parliamentarian troops under Governor William Syndenham while Portland was under the control of Royalist forces under Sir William Hastings.

On 9 February, with the help of traitors organised by one Fabian Hodder within Weymouth (including a local government councillor), the Royalists under Hastings launched a surprise attack which took control of Nothe and Chapel forts, which effectively gave them control of the town. Their small force had been secretly ferried across the narrow strait from Portland (now crossed every day by hundreds of vehicles over the Portland Road Bridge) into town where they met up with the local rebels. Their password to recognise each other was 'Crabchurch' (hence the informal title of their conspiracy) and they wore white cloths on their sleeves.

Royalist forces arrived in strength from Portland the following morning and took control of the town. The Parliamentarian forces withdrew to Melcombe, which was only linked to Weymouth town at this time by a drawbridge. Both sides bombarded each other from either side of what is now Radipole Lake and the harbour. It was during this phase that the cannonball ended up in the wall. Two weeks of combat followed in which local sources place the death toll in the hundreds.

A particularly bloody battle for the Parliamentarian forces took place on the Old High Street which used to run behind North Quay. Despite heavy casualties on both sides the Parliamentarian forces were finally victorious and the Royalists were forced to withdraw. Much to the relief of Parliament a Royalist army at Dorchester did not intervene until too late.

The cannonball itself was left wedged in the wall after the battles as a reminder of the action. The cannonball proper is believed to have been replaced by a wooden replica in case it should fall on a passersby.

The Maiden Street cannonball has allegedly been replaced by a wooden copy.

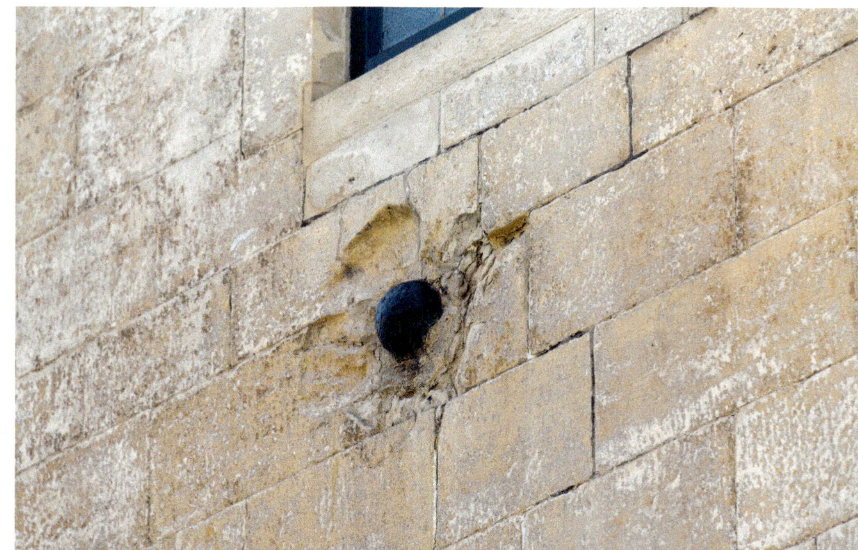

Chesil Beach

Chesil beach (also known as Chesil Bank) is an 18-mile-long shingle beach structure clearly visible from the top of the Isle of Portland and on your right as you approach Portland along the causeway. In places it is 50 feet high and over 600 feet wide. It stretches from the Isle of Portland to West Bay Pier (which effectively prevents any further movement by the pebbles in that direction). It joins the Isle or Portland to the mainland and encloses the Fleet Lagoon, creating what in geological terms is known as a tombolo.

The name Chesil is derived from the Old English word *cisel*, which means gravel. According to current geological opinions the beach formation contains around 180 billion pebbles, all regularly moved around by tide and storm, and if removed by storm often redeposited by later tide action. It is considered to have reached it's current form some 5,000 years ago

It is listed as a World Heritage Site by UNESCO and nicknamed 'Dead Man's Bay' by the writer Thomas Hardy after the numerous shipwrecks that have occurred there. The novel *Moonfleet* is set in this area, the fictional village of Moonfleet being rumoured to have been based on the village of Fleet itself.

The erection of the Portland Bill Lighthouse put an end to many of these shipwrecks but this is still considered a dangerous part of the coast, as evidenced by the large number of callouts to the RNLI lifeboat in Weymouth and the search and rescue air services.

Opinion is still divided as to how this remarkable geological feature was formed but currently the favoured one is that it was produced by the movement of sandy deposits from Lyme Bay following the rapid rise in water levels after the last ice age. These

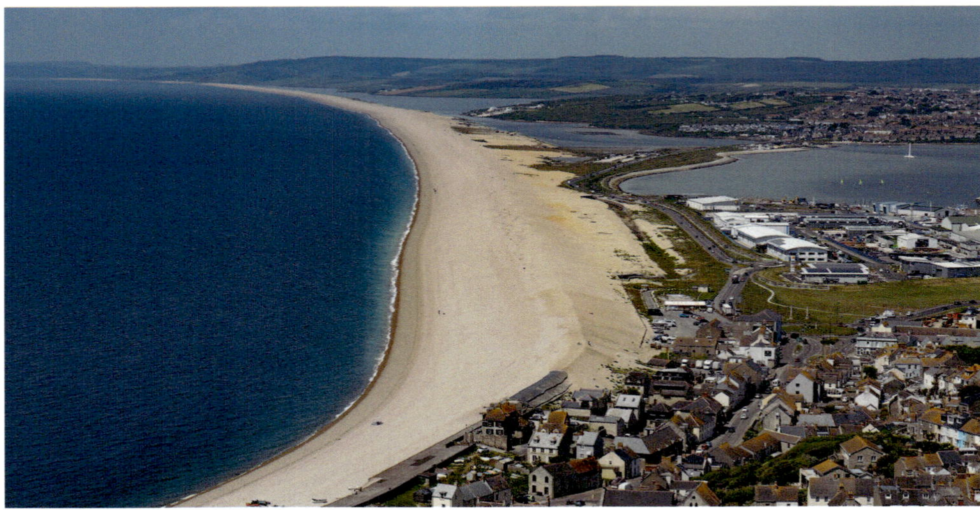

The wide sweep of Chesil beach stretching from Portland to West Bay.

deposits were driven towards the shore by the prevailing tides and formed a barrier beach, the deposits sitting on top of existing sedimentary ones. When the new, higher sea levels reached cliffs in east Devon left inland by the ice age reduction in water levels they supplied a vast amount of material (some say as much a 60 million tons) that found it's way into the structure we now call Chesil beach via the tidal operation of longshore drift.

There is a remarkable difference in pebble sizes along Chesil beach. At the West Bay end they are around the size of a pea, gradually increasing along the length of the beach to around 2 inches across at the Portland end. These pebbles are composed of a mix of flint and chert, with a scattering of less common quartzite. This supports the theory of natural tidal deposition and movement as there are no intervening man-made flood defences to disturb this natural sorting of the constituents. Legend has it that in the days of smuggling in the area smugglers could tell where they had come ashore by the size of the pebbles.

The beach currently provides very welcome protection to Weymouth and surrounding coastal villages from storms and high water, and is currently slowly being moved towards the main coastline by tidal forces. Recently a flood channel was dug to the rear of the beach to make the protection offered by the beach even greater, and to prevent flooding of the causeway.

The waterways around Chesil beach have been a Royal Engineers training ground for troops to learn bridge building from 1928 and they are still there today, although the technology has changed somewhat. During the Second World War the military came to Chesil beach and established a long rifle range and placed defensive tank traps and pill boxes in the area which can still be seen today.

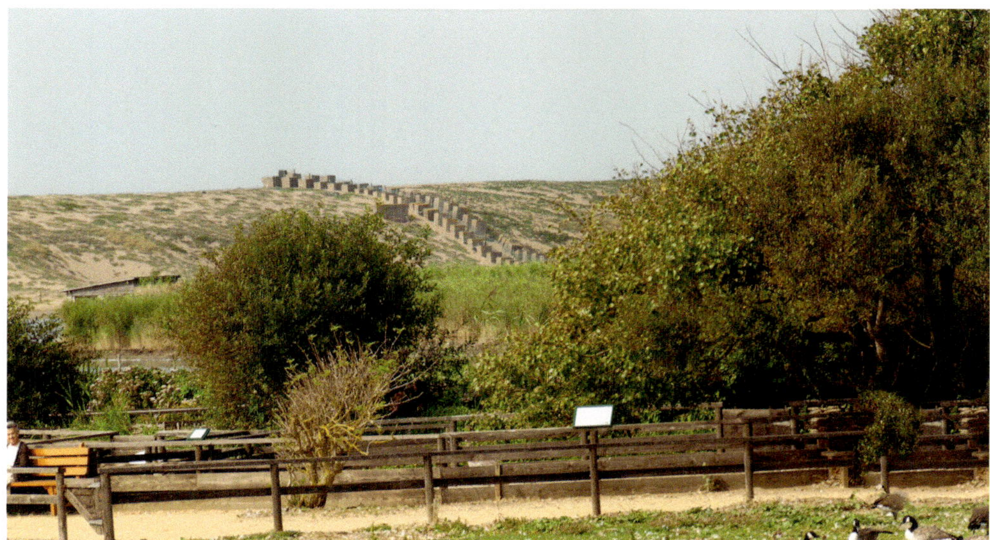

Tank traps remain on Chesil beach to this day.

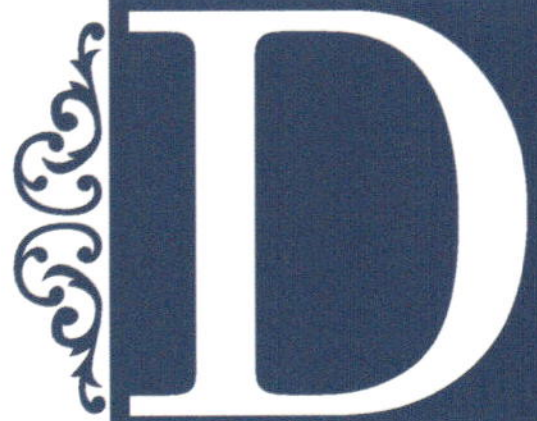

D-Day Memorial

Huge numbers of American troops passed through Weymouth during the run-up to D-Day on 6 June 1944 as Weymouth and Portland harbours were major embarkation points. Their passage is commemorated by a memorial on the Esplanade opposite the Royal Hotel.

The memorial takes the form of an art deco octagonal base and pillar of Portland stone topped by a spherical electric light that is never turned off. It is decorated with a mixture of bronze and engraved stone panels. It was unveiled on 3 December 1947 by Alderman A. P. Burt JP, Mayor, and designed by architect G. C. Wilkins LRIBA.

One plaque remembers the tragic loss of 749 lives during a training exercise off Lyme Bay when German E-boats attacked on 28 April 1944.

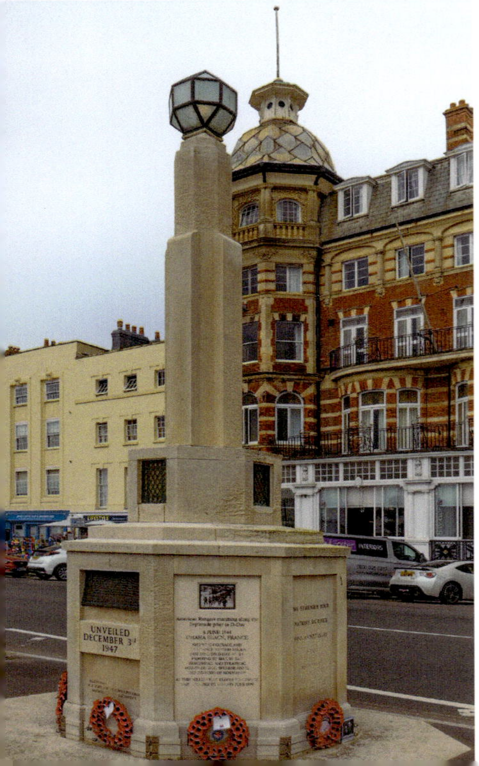

This memorial to American soldiers of D-Day stands opposite the Royal Hotel.

Plaque two is the original bronze plaque presented by the 14th Major Port, US Army and details the number of American servicemen who passed through Weymouth. According to the plaque, between 6 June 1944 and the end of the war in Europe on 7 May 1945 no fewer than 517,818 soldiers and 114,093 vehicles had passed through Weymouth on their way to Normandy. The plaque is listed as being presented by Harold G. Miller Major TC 5US, Sub Port Commander and Sherman L. Kiess Colonel, TC Port Commander.

The side referred to as plaque three shows a photograph of American Rangers marching along the Esplanade prior to embarking for the journey to Omaha beach and a tribute to their achievements. Plaque four was placed on the sixtieth anniversary of the D-Day landings. Plaque five has a remarkable and touching tribute to the Royal Navy by the American Rangers under their care.

The unusually styled monument was given listed status in 2009.

This plaque on the monument bears a touching tribute to the British Royal Navy.

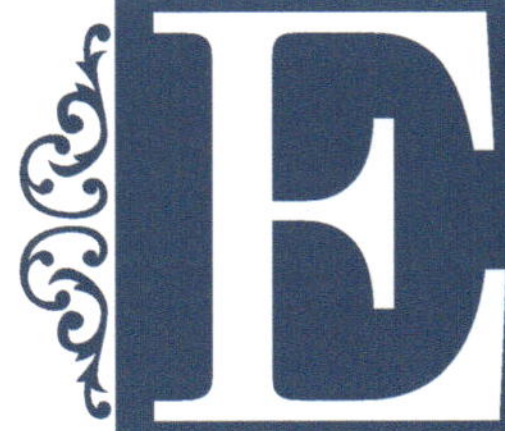

Esplanade

The word Esplanade officially means a long, open and level area upon which people can walk for pleasure. In the UK it is usually associated with being along the seafront of a tourist resort and is often used interchangeably with the similar-meaning word Promenade which means a paved place where people can walk.

Weymouth Esplanade is 1.3 miles long and stretches from Preston Road in the north to Weymouth ferry terminal in the south and every trip to Weymouth will likely involve stepping on part of it. According to Bradshaw's railway guide of 1863, Weymouth promenade is 'One of the finest marine promenades in the Kingdom.'

It is officially part of the South West Coast Path which runs from Minehead to Poole around the southern tip of the UK and, backed by a magnificent selection of Georgian and Victorian buildings, it offers wonderful views out over Weymouth Bay. There are no fewer than four war memorials, several hotels and period holidaymaker accommodation from the earliest days of Weymouth as a tourist resort.

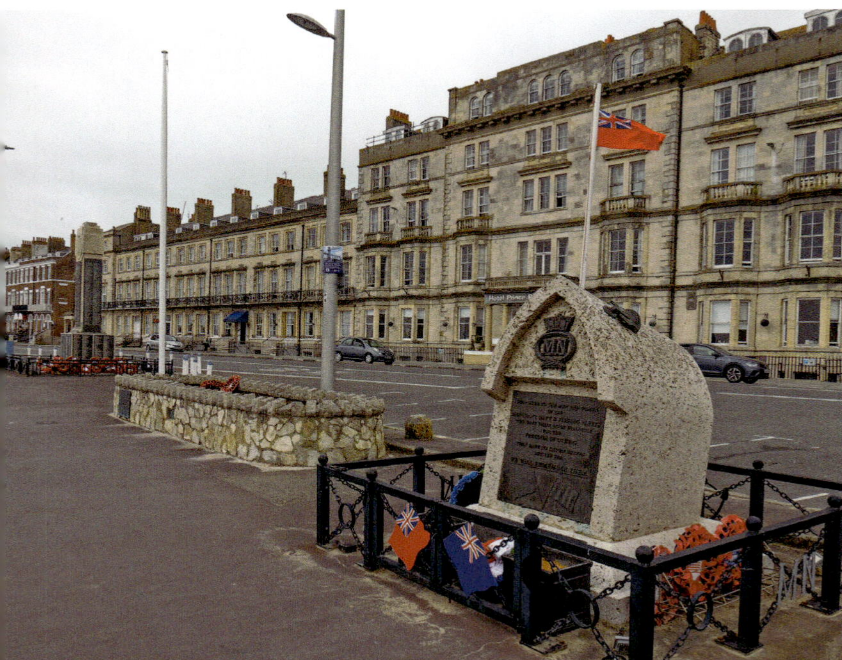

The Esplanade displays a very impressive collection of war memorials.

Fleet Lagoon

The Fleet Lagoon is a shallow salt-water lagoon created by the Chesil beach enclosure running from the Isle of Portland to West Bay. It forms the largest lagoon in England at 480 hectares. The lagoon only has a single narrow access point directly to the sea, at Ferry Bridge at the southern end.

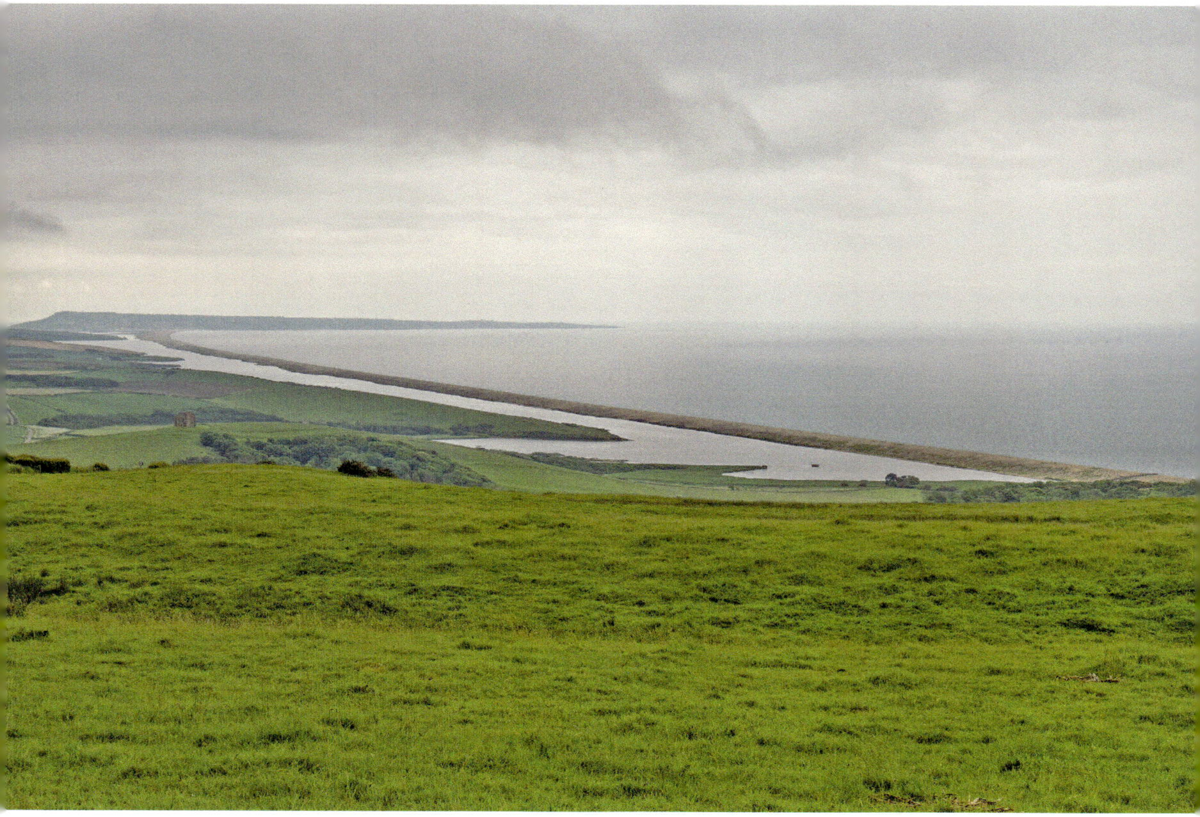

Fleet Lagoon, enclosed by the arc of Chesil beach, is England's largest lagoon.

It is best known as being the home of the Abbotsbury Swannery, the world's only managed colony of free-flying mute swans. Covering some 25 acres, keen film-goers may recognise some locations from the Harry Potter films on the site and it draws wildlife enthusiasts from all over the UK. Alongside the thousands of swans and visiting Canada geese the lagoon is home to a huge range of wildlife including the extremely rare DeFolin's lagoon snail.

During the Second World War the lagoon was used by the RAF as a bombing range and was a testing site for the famous Barnes Wallis bouncing bomb. After the war it would be used for more peaceful military work when an anchor testing station was established.

Fusee Steps

The Fusee Steps are a single flight of steep steps leading from the harbour to Nothe Gardens on Nothe headland. They were created in around 1860 and take the form of steep steps flanked by low stone walls. The tops of these walls have iron rails set mounted on them which allowed military supplies to be easily winched up from the docks to Nothe Fort on special trollies with double-flanged wheels.

They were officially given listed status as a historic landmark in 2000.

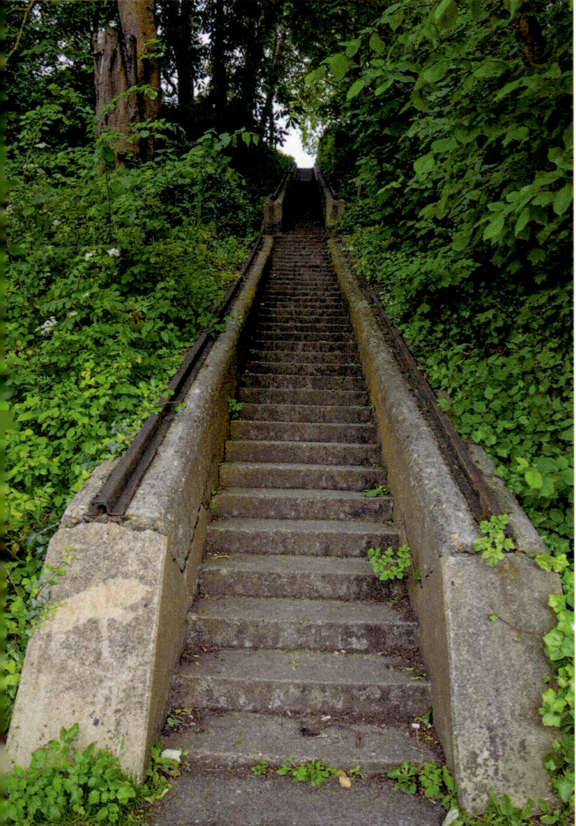

Fusee Steps showing their rails for moving heavy loads.

Greenhill Gardens

Greenhill Gardens lie at the north-eastern edge of the town in the suburb of Greenhill. They were laid out by Sir Frederick Johnstone MP in 1872 as a green space for the people of Weymouth. In 1902 Johnstone gave the gardens to the town. In 1906 he gave further land that allowed the addition of the bowls green and tennis courts that remain in use today.

The gardens slope gently from to top of the cliff to the Esplanade and are easily accessible to all through a network of gently sloping paths. Once laid out with hedges, now at the height of the season the gardens are awash with brightly coloured flower beds tended by members of local charity The Friends of Greenhill Gardens.

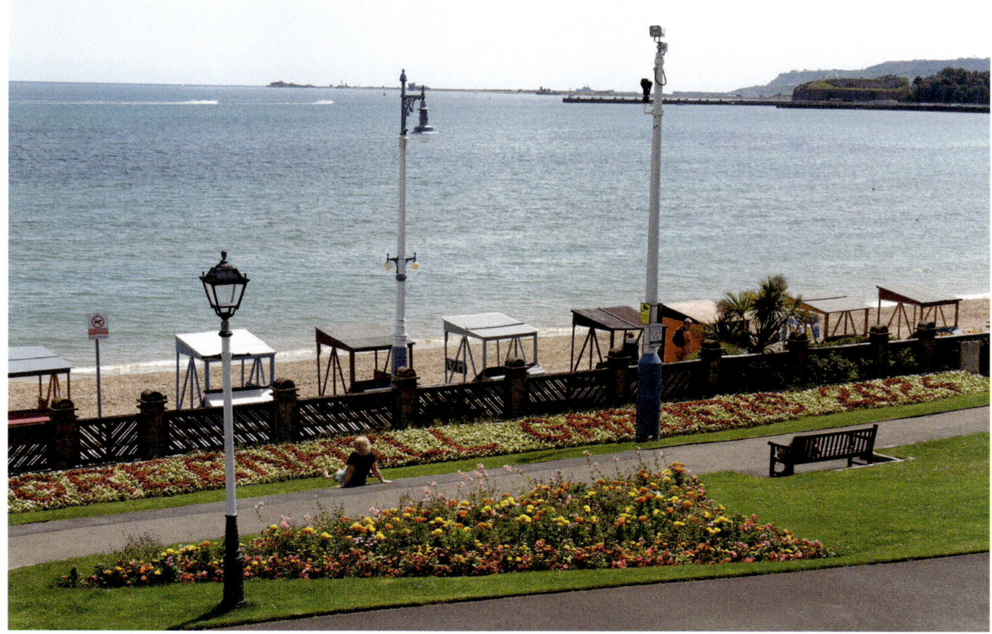

Colourful seasonal planting at Greenhill Gardens.

Bennett's Shelter for the less clement days was built in 1920 using funds donated by Mayor V. H. Bennett to mark the end of hostilities of the First World War. It was joined by unusual two-tier wooden beach huts in 1923. More normal, single-level beach huts would be built in the garden in 1929 and found fame on railway posters advertising the charms of Weymouth as a holiday destination.

1936 saw the arrival of perhaps the most memorable feature of the gardens, the floral clock. Arguably one of the last of it's kind installed in the UK, the movement was manufactured by Richie and Sons of Edinburgh and is housed in a specially built hut nearby. Most remarkably, the floral clock mechanism has an audible 'cuckoo' sound feature. Last heard many years ago, this feature has been repaired during a major overhaul of the clock mechanism during 2023 and should be heard again during the 2024 season for the first time in forty years.

Once a popular feature of the English seaside, very few of these floral clocks remain in service today.

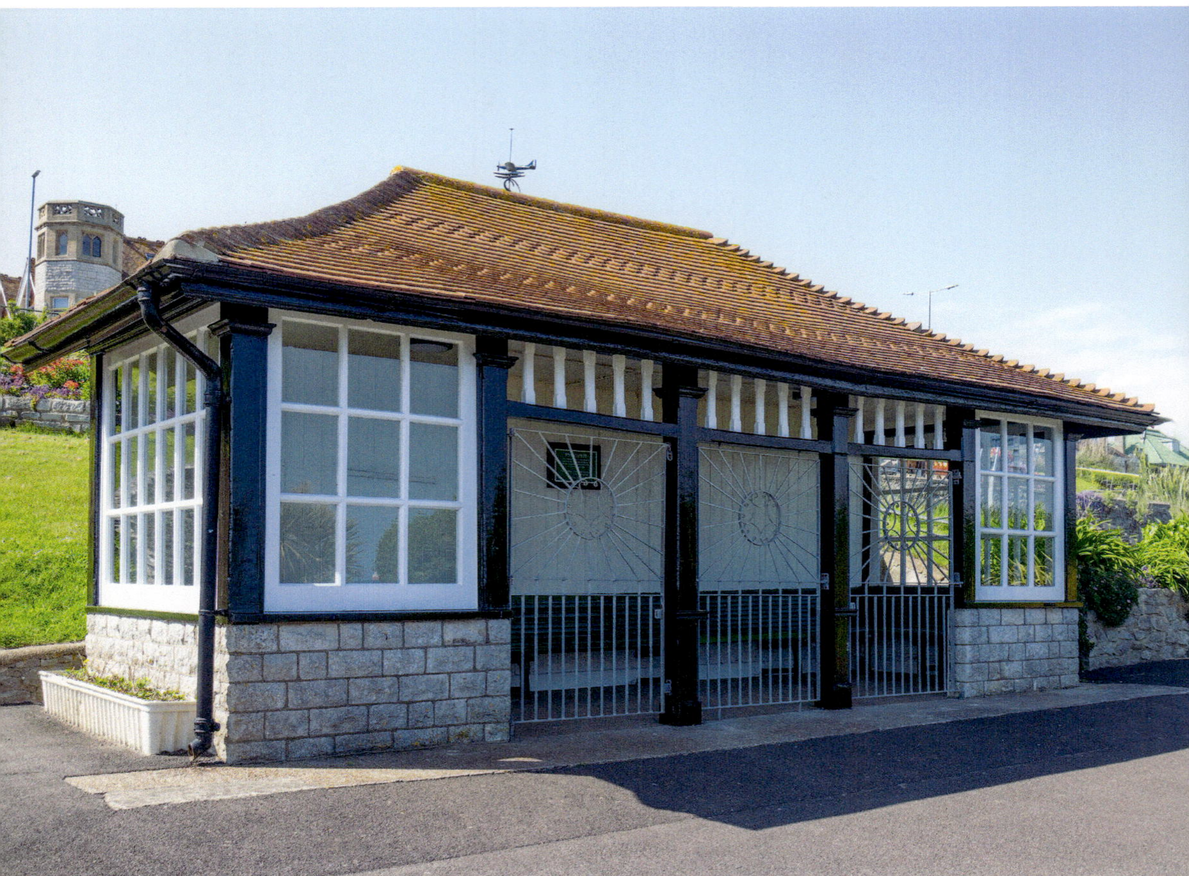

Bennett's Shelter in Greenhill Gardens dating from 1920.

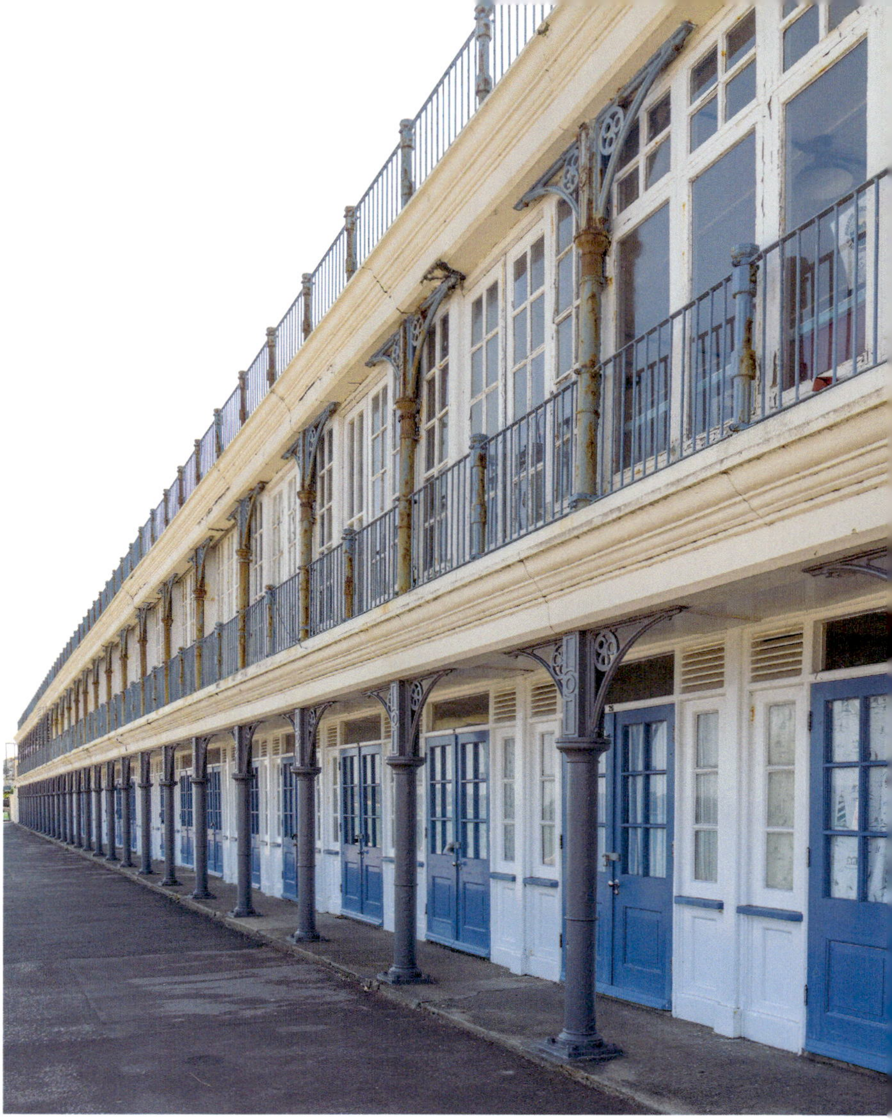

Double-level
beach huts
at Greenhill
Gardens.

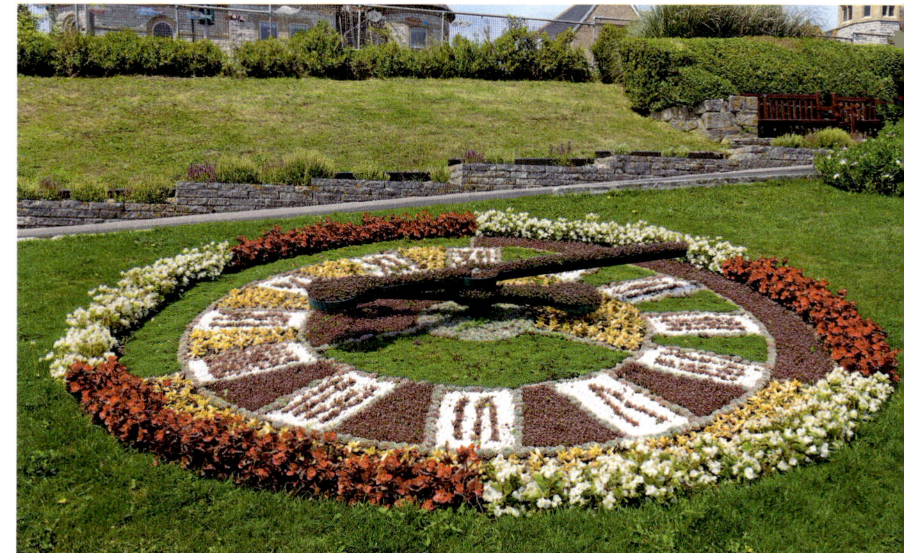

The Greenhill
Gardens floral
clock.

Alongside the floral clock, every spring a large bed in the gardens is given over to a detailed tableaux of carpet bedding commemorating a specific event. Different every year, examples have included the centenary of the end of the First World War in 2018 and all the Jubilees of Queen Elizabeth II.

Much later additions after successful fundraising were a wishing well in the 1980s and a bandstand in 2014. A magnificent new entrance arch designed by Simon Meiklejohn and Tina Walton was added in 2019 entitled 'Celebration Arch'. This was erected to honour Queen Elizabeth II and was opened by HM Lord Lieutenant of Dorset Mr Angus Campbell on 1 April 2019. It is styled to put people in mind of the look of the waves crashing on the beach in Weymouth Bay. Weighing in at over 2 tons, it is designed to have a working life of at least fifty years without needing attention.

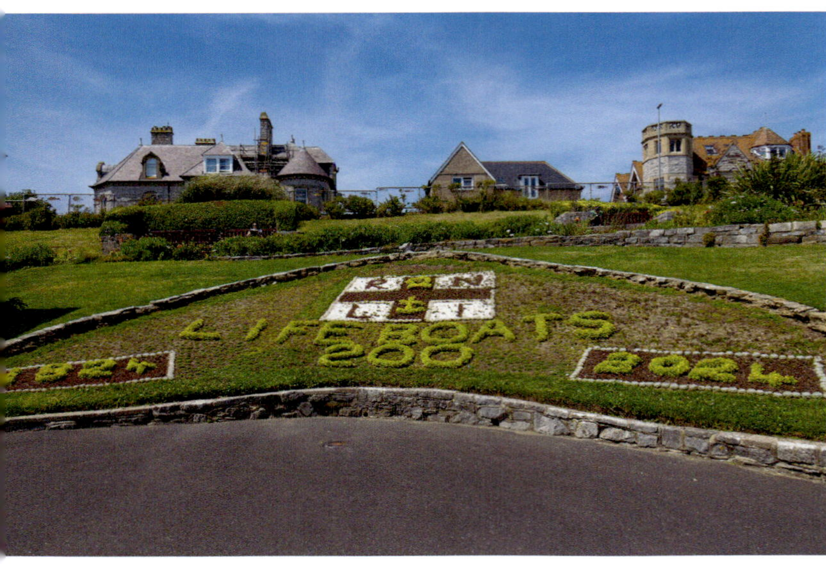

The annual commemoratory planting scheme in Greenhill Gardens.

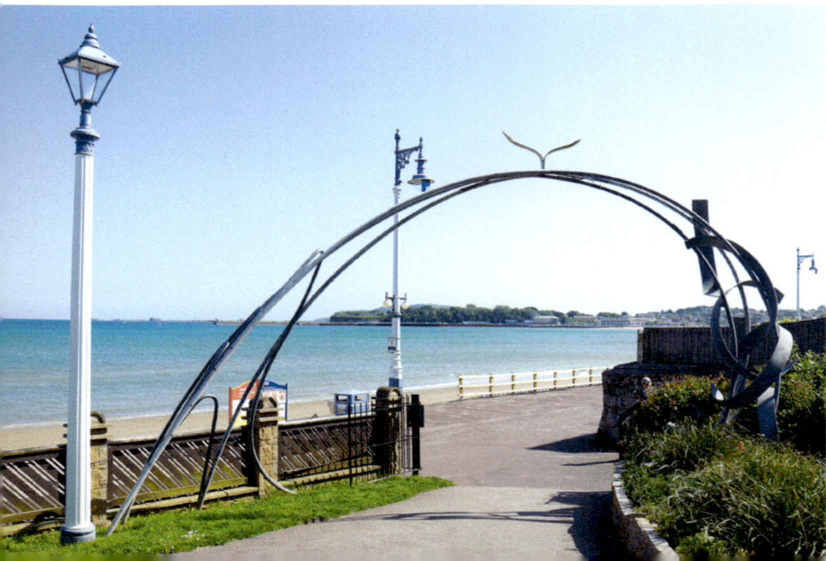

The Celebration Arch at the entrance to Greenhill Gardens, installed in 2019.

Harbour

Any visitor to Weymouth will inevitably find themselves looking down at the waters of the harbour at some stage. It is central to the town, and dates back to when what is now Weymouth was still the two separate towns of Weymouth and Melcombe Regis, one on either side of the harbour.

What is now the main part of Weymouth was Melcombe Regis and that which is on the opposite side of the harbour below Nothe Gardens was the original Weymouth.

The boroughs were officially amalgamated in 1571, although for historic reasons they continued to send four members of parliament to Westminster for many years. The Great Reform Act of 1832 reduced this number to two in total and the borough was finally abolished in 1885.

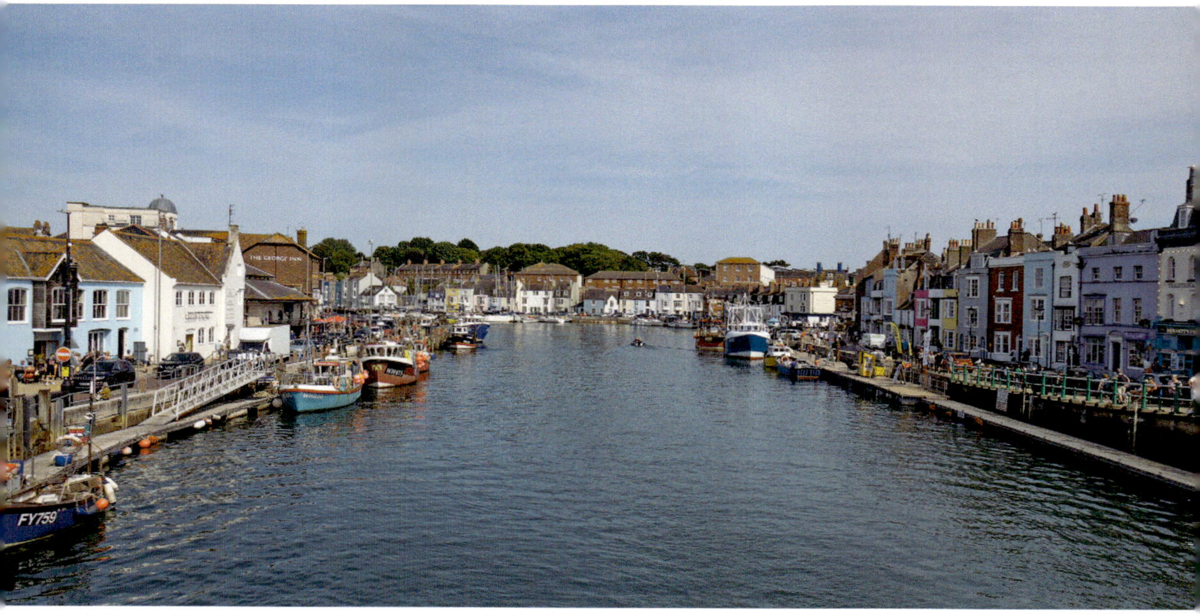

Weymouth harbour viewed from the Town Bridge looking towards the sea.

The harbour forms the mouth of the River Wey (from which Weymouth derives its name) where it exits into the English Channel. It has been a port since the days of the Roman occupation of England. In those ancient times the port was far further inland, eventually silting up to form what is now known as Radipole Lake.

The port facilities moved further down the River Wey until a fresh harbour was established at its current location, then between the towns of Melcombe Regis to the north and Weymouth Old Town to the south of the river. The colourful Town Bridge splits the harbour in two. The outer harbour is open to the English Channel, while the inner harbour, usually referred to as Weymouth Marina, offers mooring for less commercial craft and is a well-known resting place for small ships before making the crossing to France.

The marina offers mooring at four huge pontoons and all the amenities required, all only a short walk of the entertainments of the town – which goes some way to explaining its continued popularity.

The harbour is famous (or perhaps infamous would be a better term) for being the place where the plague or Black Death entered England. To the north of the harbour lies Hope Square with the old Brewers Quay building, once a brewery and now a stuttering development alongside some of the oldest buildings in Weymouth.

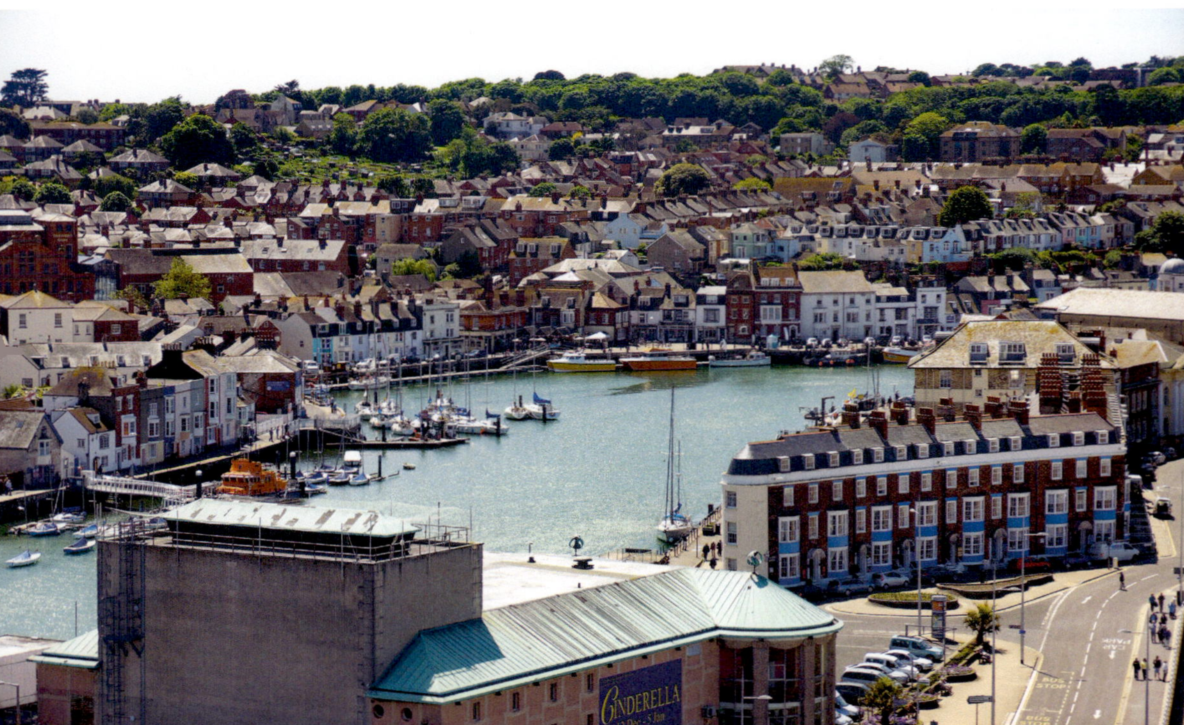

Weymouth harbour looking inland.

Alongside the main harbour but originally very much part of its commercial shipping activities is Weymouth Pier, which houses the old Channel Island ferry terminal and the Pavilion performance venue with it's monuments and giant anchor.

Records show that some sort of pier existed as early as 1812, with the beginnings of the current concrete structure being built in 1840 in the form of a pile pier formed of Portland stone debris and concrete. This would be rebuilt in 1860 and extended to a length of 900 feet from the shore with the specific purpose of landing the potato harvest from the Channel Islands.

In 1877 there was a further extension, and in 1889 a passenger-landing stage and supporting baggage hall was built to serve the Great Western Railway. Work improving the main harbour by local contractors is celebrated by an inscription on a Portland stone block near the lifeboat station marking the input of one 'John Partlett, contractor, Weymouth, 1896'.

A completely new pier structure was planned in 1930, with construction being completed in 1933 when it was officially opened by The Prince of Wales, soon to become King Edward VIII. This new pier would extend 1,300 feet out into the English Channel. During its busiest period the pier could handle three passenger vessels on the northern side while unloading three cargo ships to the south, all supported by two Great Western Railway lines.

The pier was widened again in 1971 to better serve the Channel Island ferry terminal, but a planned refurbishment in time for the sailing events of the 2012 Olympics never came to pass.

From 2012 until 2017 the pier was home to the Weymouth Sea Life (later Jurassic Skyline) Tower where people could pay to ride in a huge circular gondola which raised them 174 feet above ground and slowly rotated to give them a magnificent view of the surrounding area. Built at a reported cost of 3.5 million pounds, it came to unfortunate national fame when mechanical failure stranded seventeen people at the top of the tower when the gondola would not descend. Weather conditions prevented the more mundane methods of rescue and all seventeen had to be winched to safety by coastguard helicopter. The attraction never recovered the visitor numbers after its time in the national news and did not reopen for the 2018 season, the tower being removed in 2019.

Today the harbour remains in very active use, with the Town Bridge opening every two hours to allow boating traffic to pass unhindered between the inner and outer harbours and the English Channel. The southern side of the harbour now sports two large pubs/ restaurants (The Ship with it's huge mural being the most obvious) while the northern side offers a range of fish and chips shops, tourist shops and the lifeboat station.

During the holiday season people not wanting to walk all the way back to the Town Bridge at the landward end of the harbour to cross the water can avail themselves of the Weymouth harbour ferry. At peak times as many as four small Clinker-built rowboats operate this ferry service offering the journey across and allowing their passengers to see the harbour from a more nautical perspective.

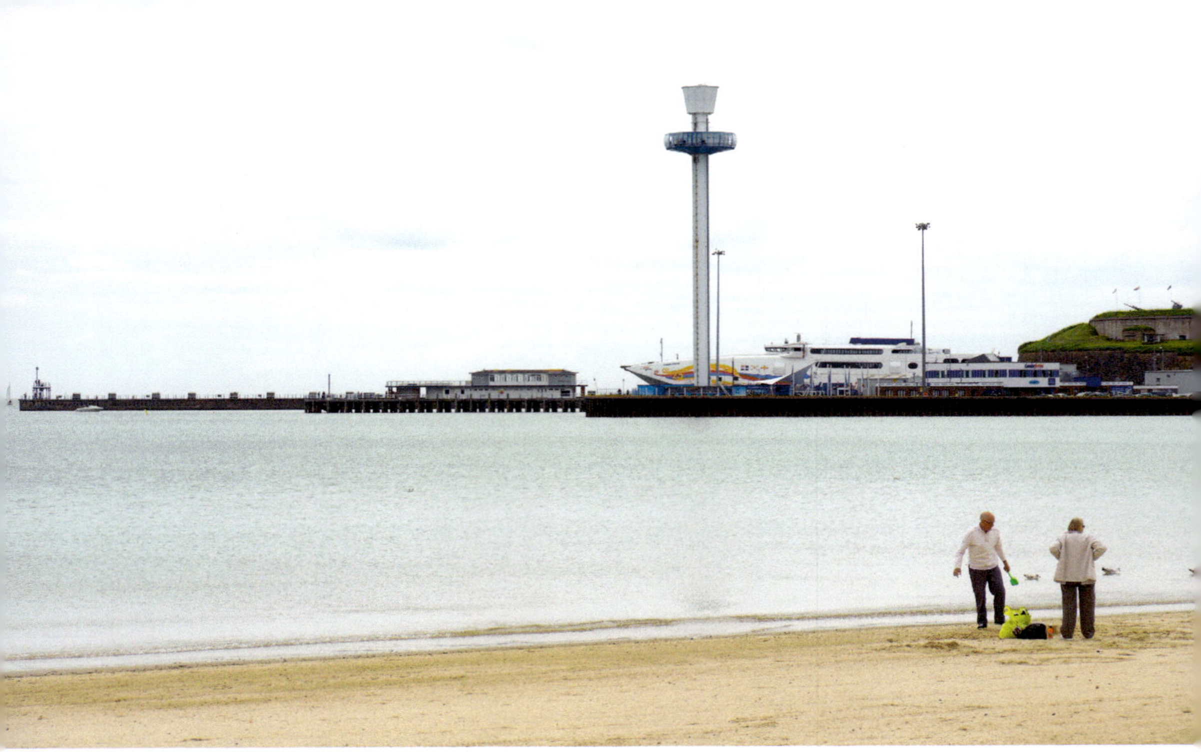

Above: The ill-fated Skyline Tower.

Below: The bridge opens every two hours to allow tall-masted craft to pass.

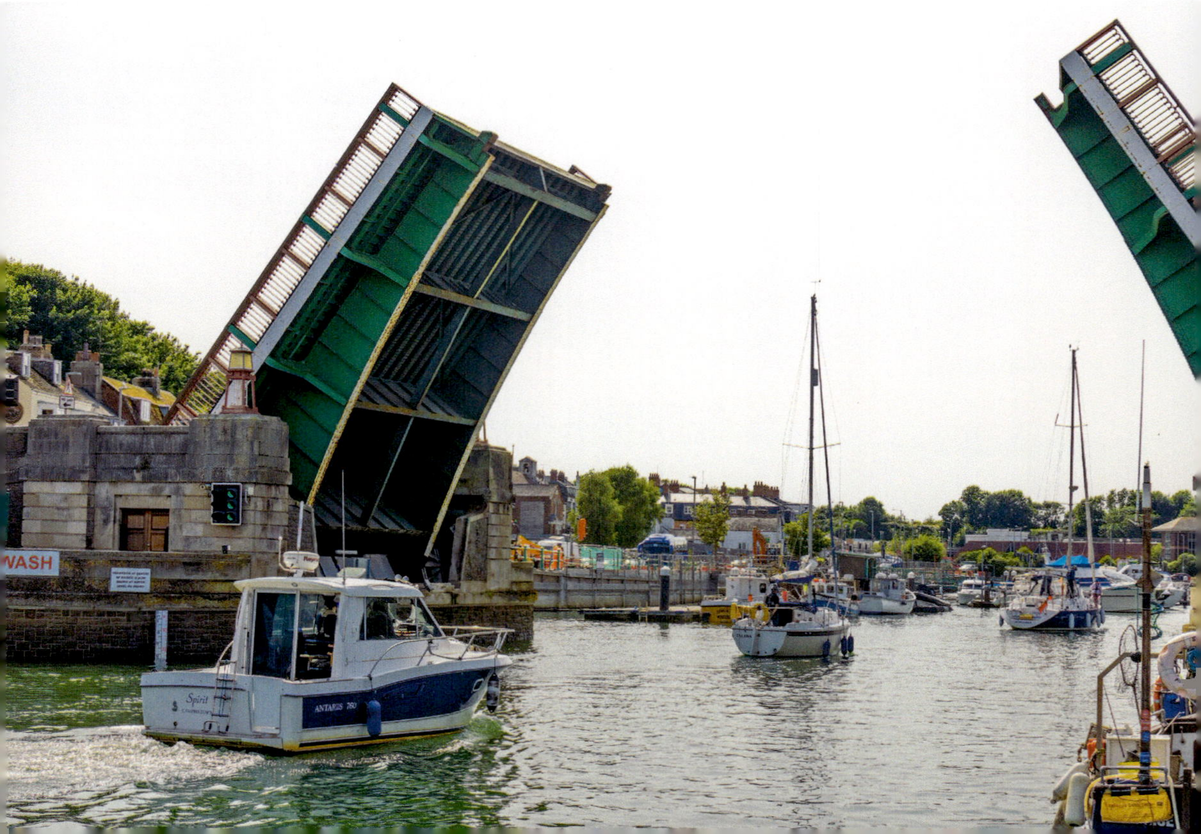

Henry Edwards Statue

The statue of Henry Edwards stands in Alexandra Gardens at the southern end of the Esplanade where the road splits in two. The figure looks out over Weymouth Bay and the beach. It celebrates a man described as the 'greatest benefactor in Weymouth's history'.

Henry Edwards was the Liberal member of parliament for Weymouth and Melcombe Regis from 1867–85 when the Borough ceased to exist. He is most famous for his charitable works and donations towards the poor, elderly and the homeless of the town.

His generous gifts to the town can still be seen in the form of ten cottages known as 'Edwardsville' on Rodwell Avenue and at Edwards Avenue on Boot Hill. These residences are still managed by the charity he set up, and every year the residents and elderly of Weymouth are still invited to an annual meal arranged by the charity, known as the Edwards Dinner Gift.

Beyond this Edwards also had built and furnished a magnificent building for the Weymouth and Melcombe Regis working men's club on Mitchell Street in 1873 which remains in use to this day.

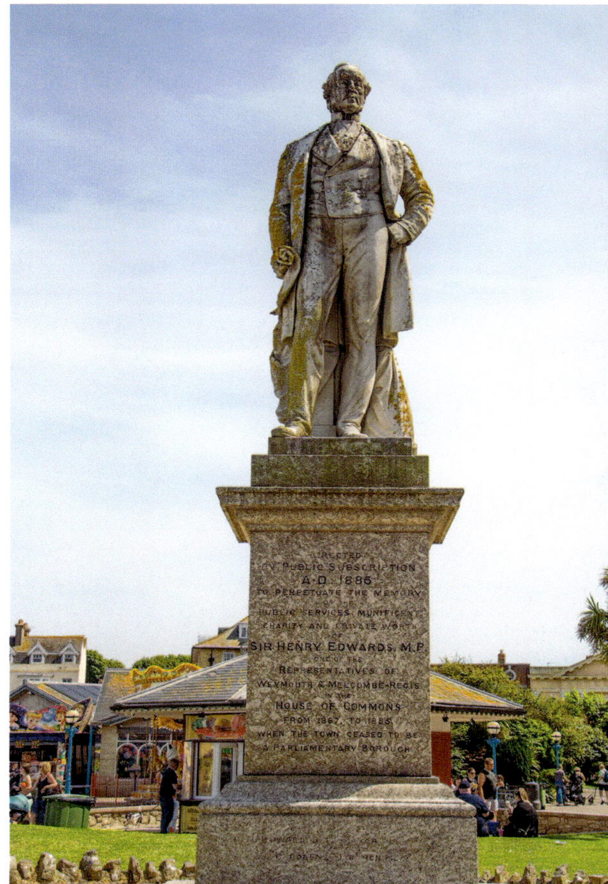

The Sir Henry Edwards statue in Alexandra Gardens.

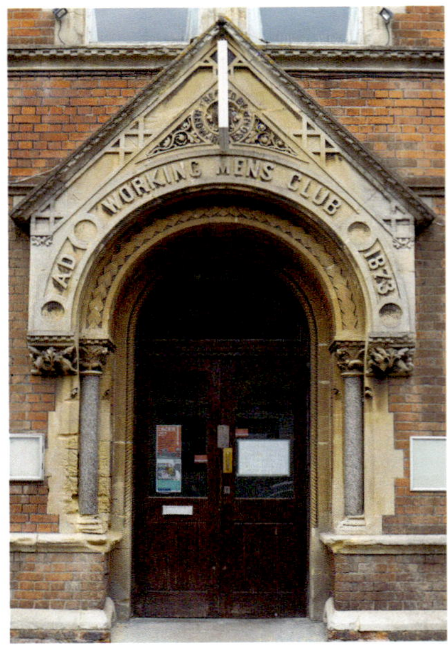

The working men's club founded by Henry Edwards in 1873.

While not being the only statue erected in his memory (another once stood in the grounds of 'Edwardsville'), this monument, erected in 1886 and paid for entirely by public subscription, remains the best-known and most obvious to a man Weymouth has good reason to celebrate. According to the inscription on the statue, it was raised to 'perpetuate the memory of the public services, munificent charity and public worth of Sir Henry Edwards MP'. Following his time as an MP he was offered the Freedom of the Borough, but chose to decline the honour.

He died in London after a long illness in 1885 and is buried in Melcombe Regis cemetery.

Hope United Reformed Church

If you should look upwards while on Trinity Street you will see the magnificent front architecture of the Hope United Reformed Church. Originally known as the Hope Congregational Chapel, this free-standing building was constructed in the early 1860s on the site of an earlier 1822 chapel. Like many of the fine buildings of Weymouth, the Hope United as it stands today is constructed of Portland stone with a brick dressing and a slate roof.

An independent congregation of the United Reformed Church (a branch of Methodism) was formed in 1817 on the Weymouth side of the busy harbour. A private house was converted to cover the needs of 100 worshipers. The church congregation was officially founded in November 1821 and fundraising was immediately started for the construction of a purpose-built chapel.

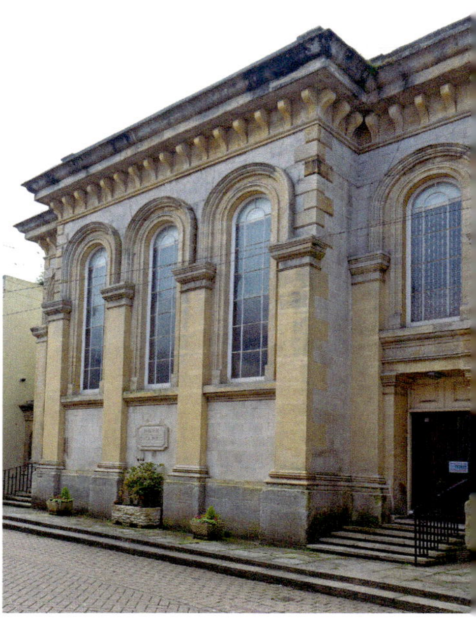

Hope Congregational Chapel on Trinity Street.

A suitable plot of land was leased from Sir Frederick Johnstone and the new chapel was swiftly created and ready for use by 21 August 1822. The congregation thrived and the building was enlarged in 1833 and an organ installed. In 1859 the organ was refurbished and enlarged by Bevington and Son of London for the princely sum of £130.

By 1860 the congregation had once again outgrown the existing building and in 1860 plans were afoot to build a new chapel on the same site. The search was on for a builder, and tenders were invited in February 1861. In the spirit of being a local organisation the accepted tender was from a Mr A. Williams of Weymouth, the grandson of the builder involved in the construction of the original building. His bill for the new erection was £1,144.

The foundation stone of the new chapel was laid on 3 April 1866 by Matthew Devenish of Dorchester and the congregation made themselves at home at the Congregational Chapel in nearby Nicholas Street while the building works took place.

Public worship began again in January 1862 while building works were still ongoing. The new chapel was officially dedicated on 5 March 1862 when the Reverend G. Smith of Poplar preached in the morning and the Reverend H. B. of Islington preached in the afternoon.

In 1871 the Johnstone estate handed the church the freehold of the land upon which the chapel was built. In 1873 11 St Leonards Terrace was purchased by the chapel as a home for the minister.

With a rapidly growing local population, the chapel schoolroom was soon overcrowded and land was purchased for a new, larger schoolroom at the rear of the chapel building. The foundation stone was laid by Mayor R. N. Howard on 11 November 1885 and the red-brick schoolroom was completed and ready for use on 21 April 1886 at the cost of £1,000.

Ice Cream

No traditional trip to the English seaside would be complete without an ice cream. This was a Victorian custom that started out as the 'penny lick' where people paid their copper penny and were handed a glass to hold with a shallow depression in the top into which a small amount of ice cream was applied and they licked it off. The glass was then handed back to the vendor and it was often used again straightaway with no thought to hygiene.

While there are many places in Weymouth that will happily supply you with a simple ice cream, most famous among them is the prominent and nationally famous Rossi's ice cream parlour on the Esplanade.

Established in 1937 by Fioravanti Figliolini in what was the Royal Arcade building, it still provides a fine selection of hand-made ice cream flavours made daily to what is described as a 'closely guarded family recipe'. Long an ice cream landmark and bearing a very prominent art deco store frontage under the architectural magnificence of the Royal Arcade on the Esplanade, Rossi's even found themselves selling ice cream to visiting American soldiers during the Second World War.

Rossi's leapt to national fame when they were visited by the television travel show *Susan Calman's Grand Day Out* in 2022. Her lengthy profile and visit of the store ensured that for all of 2022 there were longer queues at Rossi's than ever.

Founder Fioravanti passed away in 1971 and his son Eugenio took over the business, passing it along in turn to the third generation of the family in 1976. Currently owned by Fulvio Figliolini (known locally as 'Figgy'), he has recently been joined by his daughter Aimee in the family business. Long may their distinctive business on the Esplanade continue to flourish.

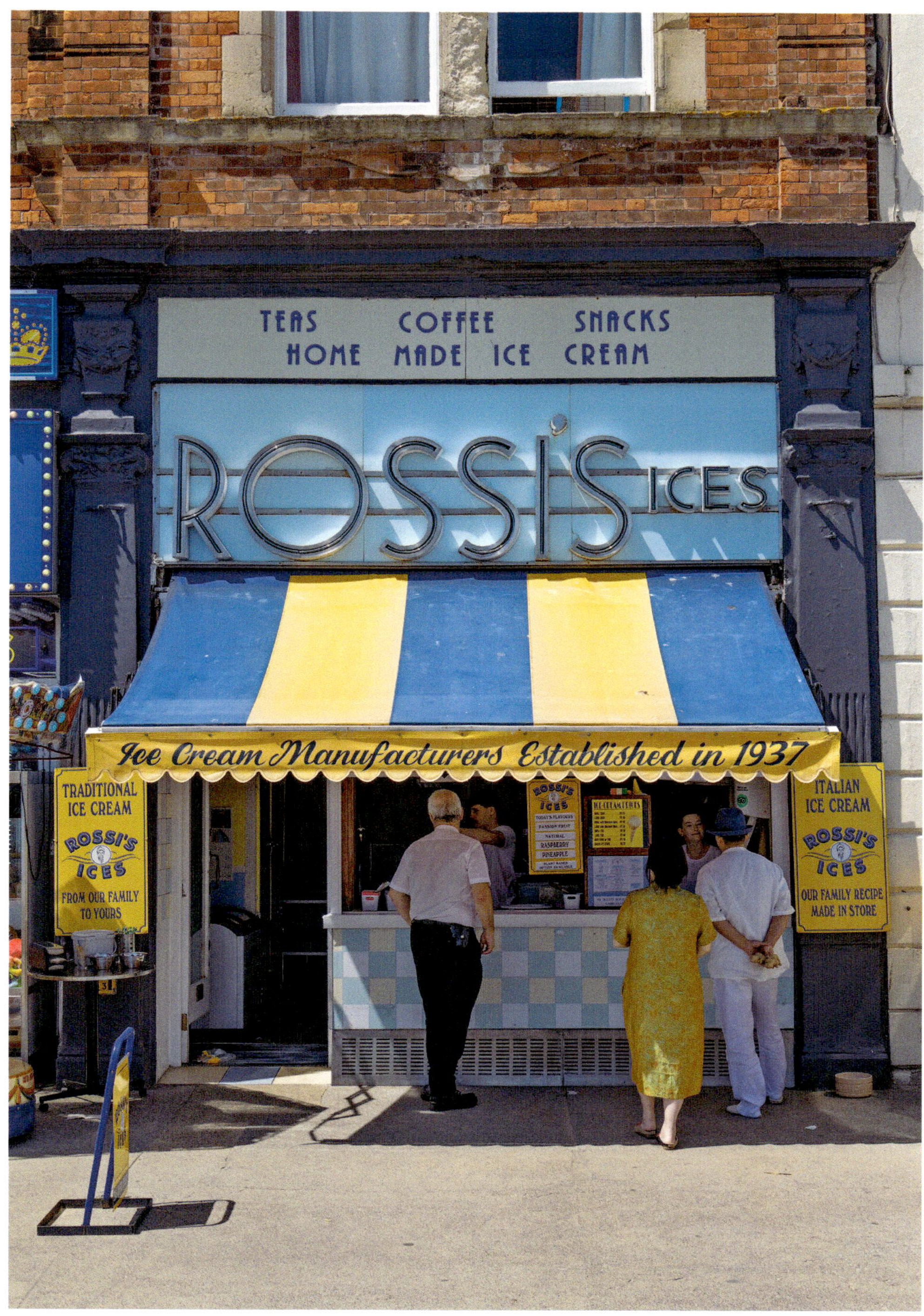

Rossi's ice-cream parlour in the Royal Arcade.

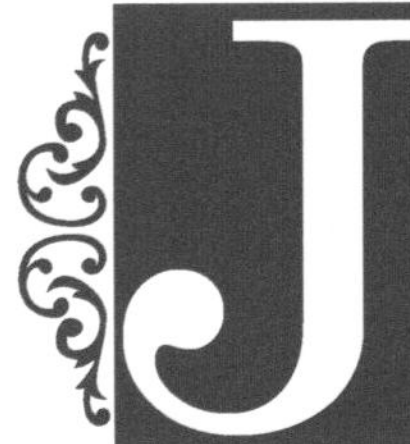

Jubilee Clock Tower

If you walk along the Esplanade near the junction with King Street you will be rewarded by the sight of what must be one of Weymouth's best-known landmarks, the gloriously colourful Queen Victoria Jubilee Clock Tower, a 'florid but characteristic enrichment to the seafront, boldly coloured', according to the Historic England listing description.

It was unveiled by Mayor John Groves on 31 October 1888 to celebrate the 1887 Golden Jubilee of the reign of Queen Victoria.

The funds for the clock were raised by public subscription, the bulk of said subscription being raised during the actual Jubilee Day celebrations on 21 June 1887. After the payment of expenses for the revelries of the day itself, £100 remained in the fund and the council was approached with the idea of putting this towards a more permanent memorial to the Jubilee.

The structure is constructed of a mixture of cast and wrought iron standing on a mounting of Portland stone supplied by the Weymouth Corporation. Designed by the headmaster of the local school of art, Mr Baker, each side has two panels alternating with the head in profile of Queen Victoria and the coat of arms of Weymouth.

Sadly the funds raised were only sufficient for the basic structure and the clock, with four illuminated faces, manufactured by Thwaites & Reid of London, was donated to the tower by Sir Henry Edwards whose statue stands at the other end of the Esplanade and whose generosity to the town is detailed elsewhere. The Weymouth Gas Company was persuaded to ensure the clock faces would be illuminated 'in perpetuity free of charge'.

Originally standing on a small physical extension of the Esplanade out into the sands of the beach, the 1920s would see a major expansion of the Esplanade on the seaward side of the clock to the shape you see today.

These major works all along the seafront at this time were part of a nationwide 'Public Works' scheme sponsored by the Liberal government in response to the massive unemployment that followed the return of demobilised men from the First World War. The government paid the bulk of the wages of the workers employed in these schemes, bringing work to 500 local labourers.

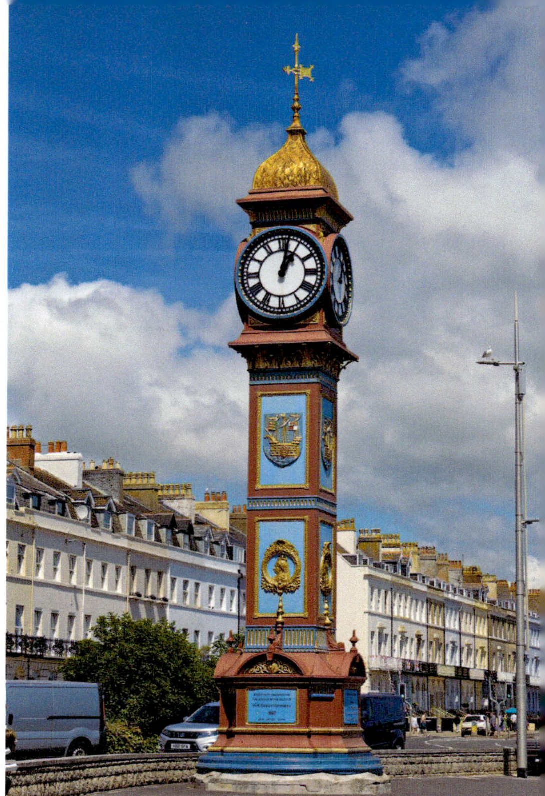

The Weymouth Jubilee Clock Tower, first unveiled in 1888.

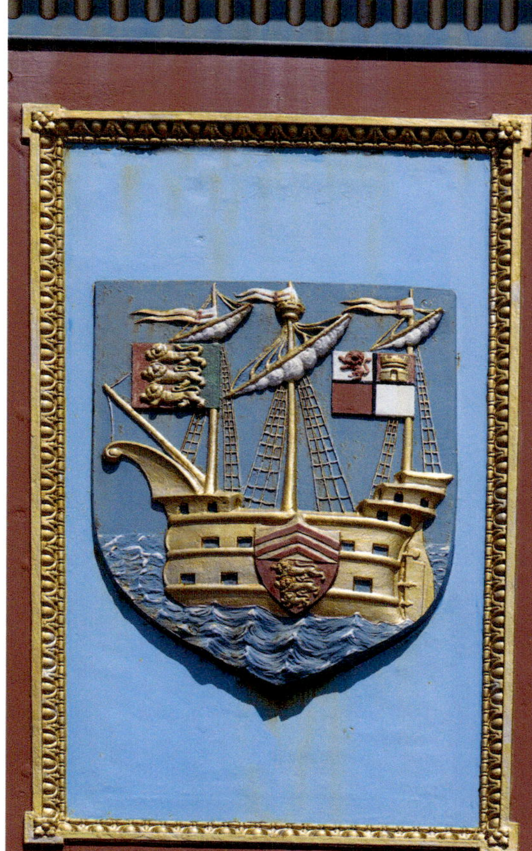

A detail of the coat of arms of Weymouth on the Jubilee Clock Tower.

Originally displayed in its native metallic shades, when the Esplanade was extended on the seaward side of the clock in the 1920s the bright Weymouth town colours you see it wearing today were applied and have remained ever since. The clock was given historic listed status in this form in June 1974.

The clock itself was refurbished and the tower received a major repaint and re-gilding in 2011 in preparation for the huge influx of tourists expected for the Olympics in 2012.

Jurassic Coast

Weymouth sits loosely at the centre of the Jurassic Coast. Famous all over the world, it stretches for approximately 95 miles from Swanage to Exmouth. Drawing visitors from all over the world is its famous rock formations, red cliffs, red sand and fossils.

It is the only place in the world where a geologist can view rocks from the Jurassic, Triassic and Cretaceous periods together. The timescale covered by those periods covers no less than 185 five million yeas of the Earth's history.

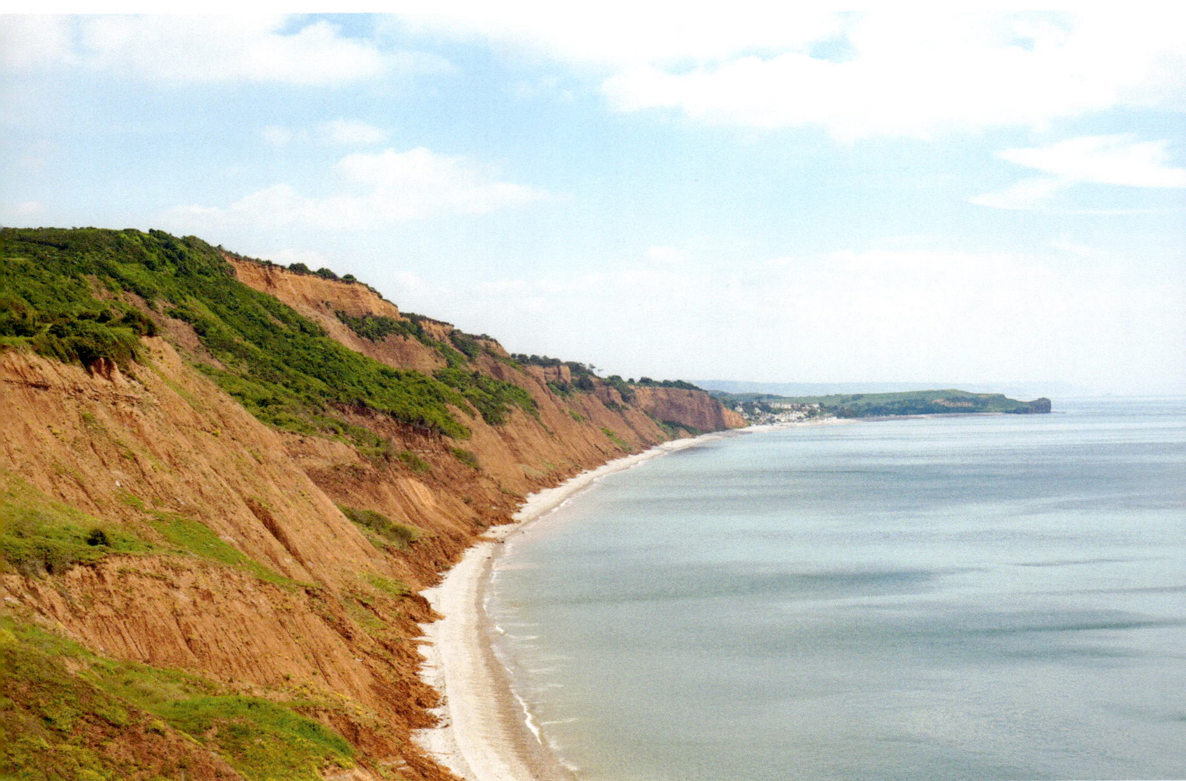

The tall, red cliffs and sand that characterise the Jurassic Coast.

King George Statue

The fame and growth of Weymouth as a bathing and tourist resort during Georgian times can be entirely traced to the patronage of King George III. His many visits to take the water, starting from 1789, brought Weymouth to the notice of the rest of England. The lines of Georgian period buildings all along the Esplanade pay tribute to the speed with which Weymouth grew under his patronage. Small wonder then that the largest statue on Weymouth seafront is its tribute to this king.

Situated where the Esplanade forms a loop creating a traffic island and giving its name to the nearby public toilets (yes, they are officially known as the King's Statue public toilets), the imposing statue dominates this end of Weymouth's seafront.

The plan to build a statue was first considered in 1802 and the King gave permission for a statue to be erected in his honour in Weymouth. A design was accepted from the architect James Hamilton and the statue manufactured. The plan was put on hold when King George fell ill in 1805 and the statue was put into safe keeping and effectively forgotten.

In 1809 King George III entered the fiftieth year of his reign and in celebration of his Golden Jubilee the statue was taken out of storage and a foundation stone for the huge pedestal laid in the presence of two of the King's children, Adolphus, Duke of Cambridge and Princess Mary. The structure was unveiled on 25 October 1810.

The life-size statue of the king stands holding a sceptre on top of the very tall and wide pedestal of Portland stone. He is flanked by the Union Jack, the Royal Crown on a cushion, a pile of books and a large oval shield bearing his coat of arms.

The pile of books commemorates the King's Library, an institution that would become the foundation of the British Library. In these days of revisionist history, it is often forgotten that before being known as the 'Mad King', King George III was considered a notable scholar.

The base of the pedestal is flanked on either side by life-size representations of a golden lion and a (if life-size is a phrase that can be used to describe a mythical being) white unicorn, whose horn has gone missing on many occasions over the years. The dedication to the King and his Golden Jubilee is engraved on the front of the plinth and signed by the original architect.

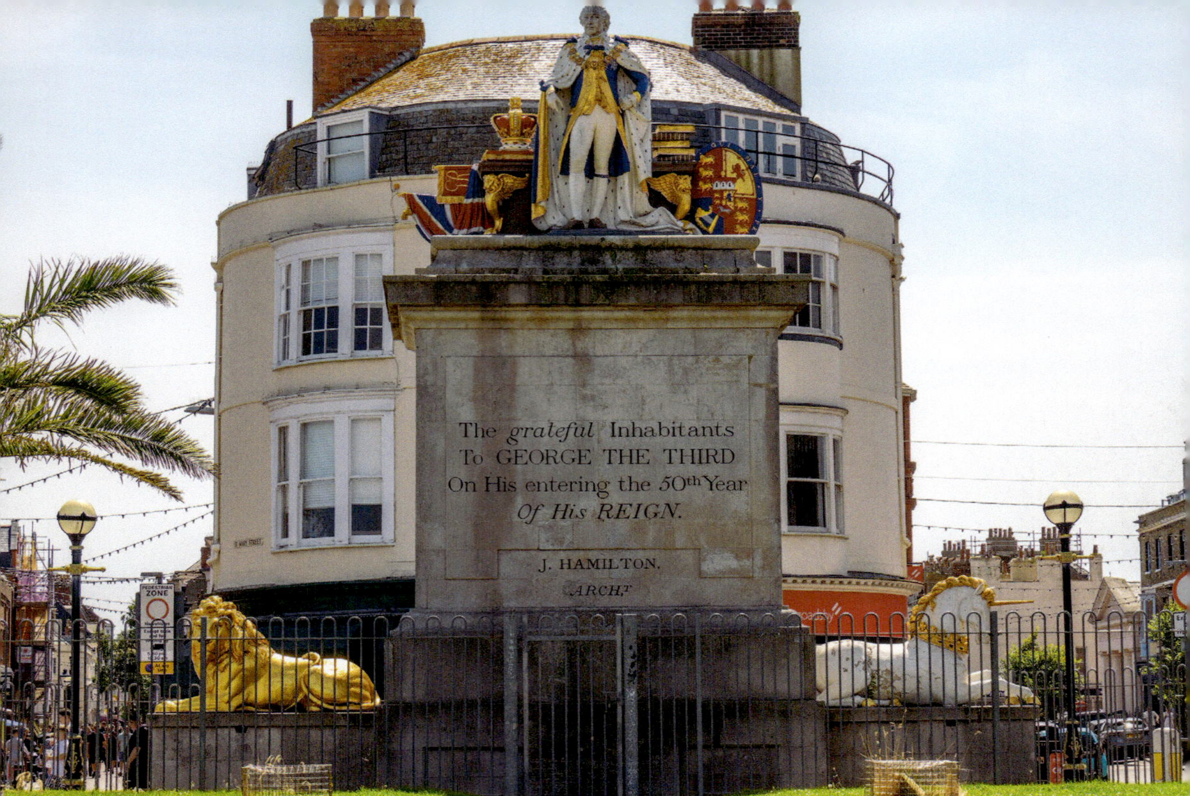

The King George III statue with flanking figures was unveiled in 1810.

Much like the Queen Victoria Jubilee Clock at the opposite end of the Esplanade, the statue was originally painted bronze, only receiving his current bright colours in 1948.

The statuary itself is cast from an unusual ceramic material known as Coade stone, invented by Mrs Elizabeth Coade, the statue itself being created at the Lambeth Ornamental stone manufactory by her company, Coade and Sealey. Curiously, Mrs Coade was not actually married but adopted the Mrs title to give the impression of respectability. She kept a house in nearby Lyme Regis.

Initially the statue was to have been erected further down the Esplanade where it would be more visible to all the buildings on the seafront, but it was eventually erected where it stands today at what was then the junction of the two largest streets on the seafront. It became a location for the celebration of events of national importance such as the end of both World Wars and the announcement of the Coronation of Queen Elizabeth II.

During the updates to road layouts during the late 1950s the statue found itself on the traffic island it still occupies today. It received listed status in December 1953.

In 2007, 200 years of accumulated dirt, no fewer than twenty layers of old paint some 5 millimetres thick and the occasional piece of vandalism were removed. Fresh paint and gold leaf was applied and today the statue dominates the southern end of the Esplanade.

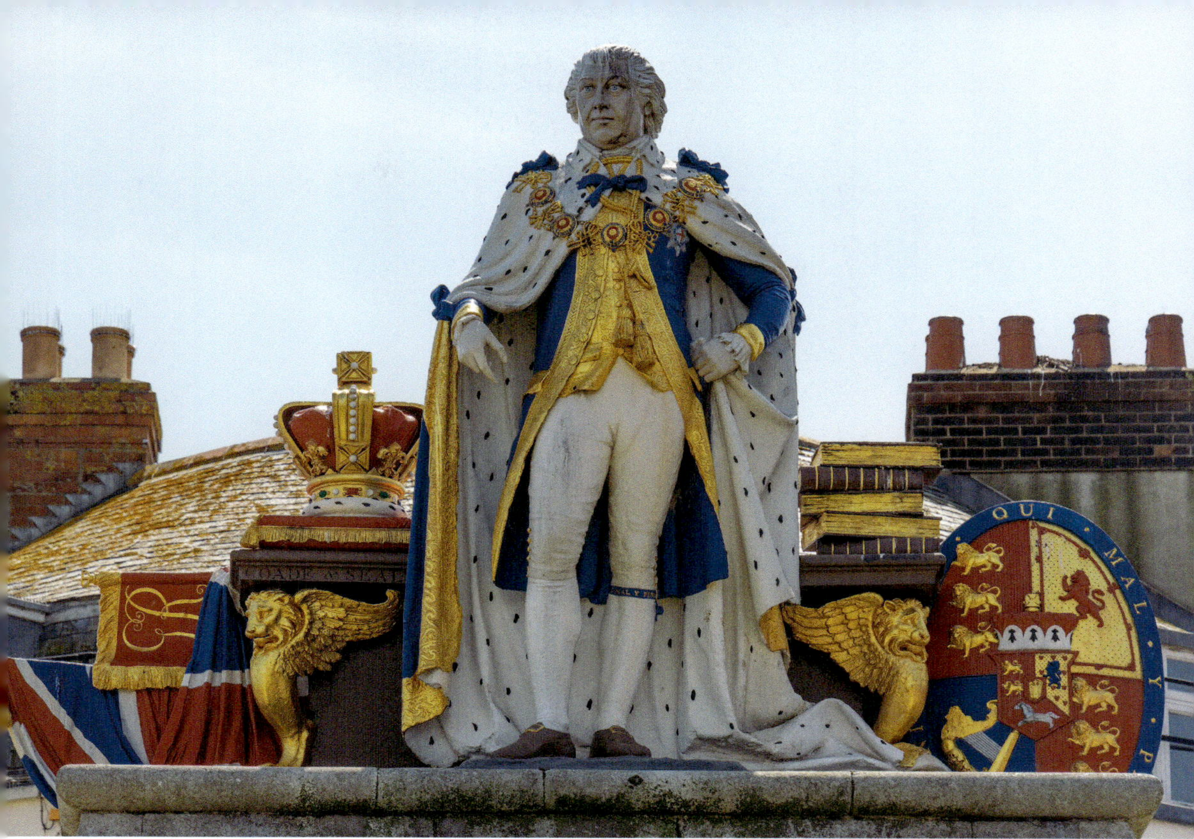

The figure of King George III flanked by book, crown and heraldic shield.

The statue has not always been universally popular, being described by one journalist writing for the *Southern Times* as 'that hideous monstrosity known as The King's Statue' while reviewing the unveiling of the statue of Sir Henry Edwardes in Alexandra Gardens nearby.

Land Train

If you visit Weymouth during the holiday season you can expect to see and hear the foremost exponent of tourist transport running up and down the Esplanade – the Weymouth land train.

Resplendent in blue, the Italian-built Dotto land train runs a continuous service between Hope Square by the harbour at the southern end of the route and the Sea Life Centre at the northern end towing a train of easily accessible carriages. Their circular route takes around thirty minutes to complete and is considered an excellent way to see many of Weymouth's better-known landmarks.

In the 2023 Dorset Tourism Awards the land train service received a Commended award for their services to tourism in the area.

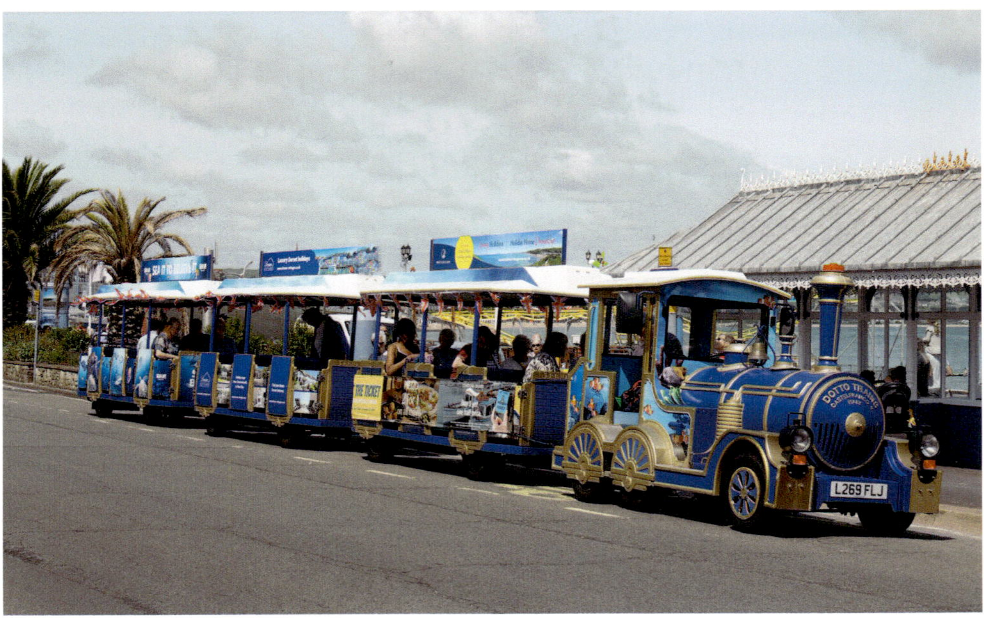

The land train offers award-winning local transport.

Levels

Installed in 2021 as part of the Weymouth art trail, 'The Levels' stands at the widest part of the Promenade on a stone plinth opposite the Jubilee Clock. The sculpture was created by Raphael Daden to raise awareness of climate change and rising sea levels.

The ever-rising sea levels of the world are represented by coloured bands of resin set within a large steel ring representing a ship's porthole. It is set atop a Portland stone plinth bearing a laser-cut poem on a steel sheet by Aly Stoneman. While standing reading the poem and admiring the artwork the viewer is supposed to find themselves inspired to look out to sea over Weymouth Bay.

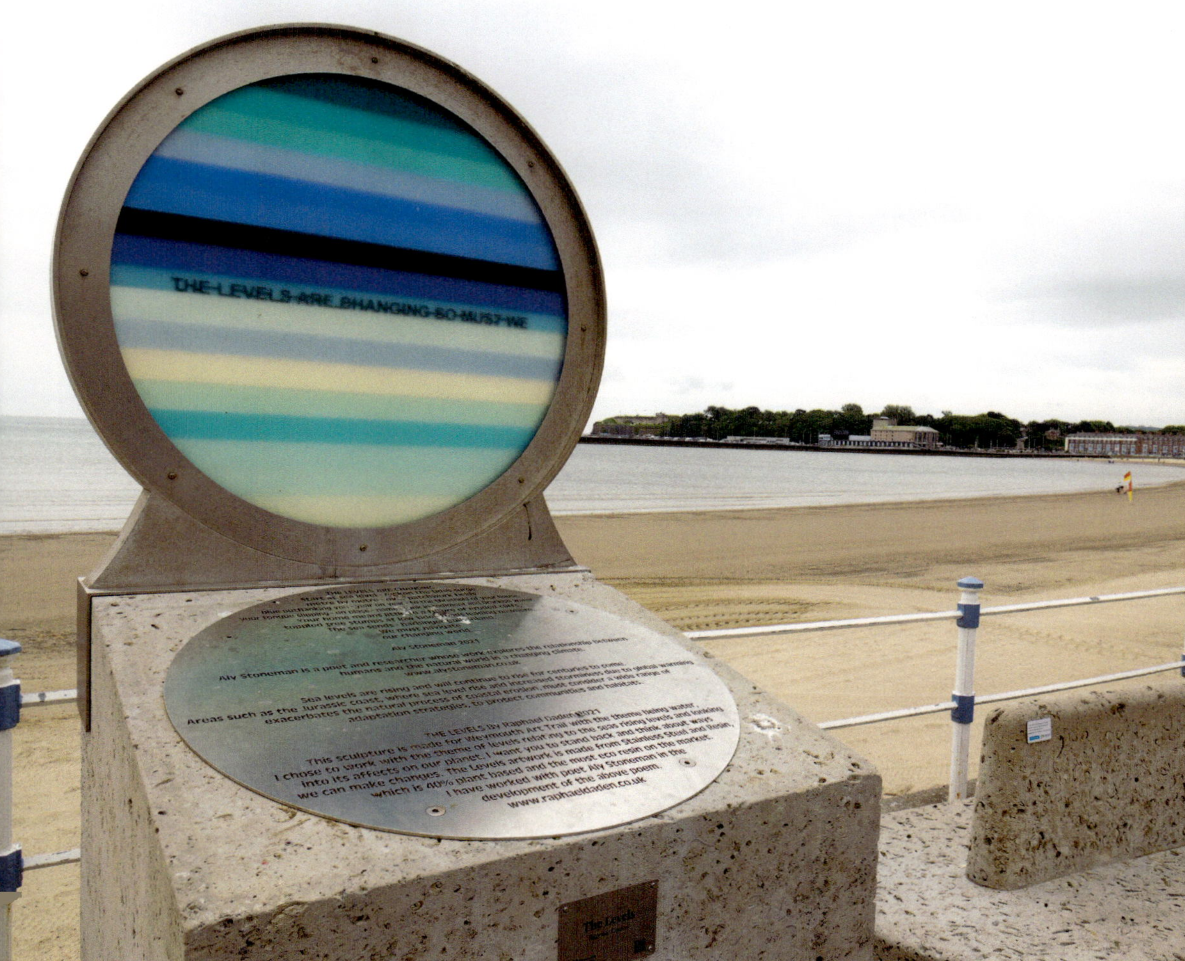

'The Levels' sculpture looking out over Weymouth Bay.

Lifeboat

If you walk along Customs Quay by the harbour and look across the water you will usually see moored there a brightly coloured lifeboat. This is the most obvious presence of the RNLI (Royal National Lifeboat Institution) in Weymouth.

The RNLI station in Weymouth was established and opened on 26 January 1869 at the request of the Earl of Strafford and is currently one of the busiest on the south coast of England.

At the time of writing they have two vessels operating from this station. A Severn class all-weather vessel named *The Ernest and Mabel* and a B class Atlantic 85 inshore called the *Jack and Phyl Cleare*.

The original boathouse was rebuilt in 1924 to house the first motor-powered lifeboat, the *Samuel Oakes*. The old crew building still remains to this day, now occupied by the RNLI fundraising gift shop. Above the door is a large bay window once used as a lookout point to watch out for ships in trouble. The date of this last modification to the building is commemorated in stone above the old boat door.

The arrival of a Barnett class lifeboat in 1930 meant the boathouse was outgrown again and an arrangement was made to allow it to be moored permanently in the harbour, a deal that continues to this day, as the photograph here shows.

When the all-weather lifeboat was joined by a lighter inshore lifeboat in 1995 a satellite boathouse was built nearer to the mouth of the harbour with its own dedicated slipway.

The stated aim of the Weymouth station is to attend any emergency within 50 miles of their location within two hours of launch. Their Severn class lifeboat has a range of 250 nautical miles and a top speed of 25 knots.

They are supported by the RNLI stations in Exmouth to the west and Swanage to the east. An inshore lifeboat also operates out of Lyme Regis which gives a weekly spirited fundraising display to the tourists during the holiday season.

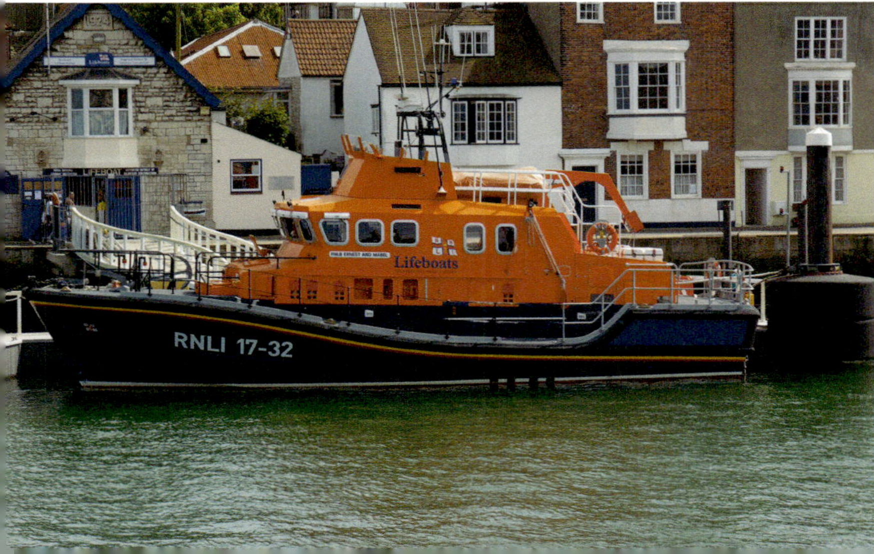

The RNLI Severn Class lifeboat based in Weymouth harbour.

Lighthouse

Portland Bill Lighthouse is located on the southernmost tip of the Isle of Portland and is a very obvious landmark as you approach, standing some 135 feet tall and painted with bright red and white horizontal stripes.

The current lighthouse was built by Trinity House in 1906 to guide and safeguard the sea traffic of Weymouth and Portland, its recently refurbished LED light throwing out a beam of some 18 nautical miles.

The conflicting tides in the area, known as the Portland Race, have caused many ships to founder in this area. Where the tides meet between Portland Bill and the Shambles sandbank some 3 miles south-east of Portland Bill a constant disturbance in the water can often be seen from shore. During the age of sail this was sufficient to drive ships ashore.

Plans for a lighthouse were proposed as early as 1669 by a Sir John Clayton. In the 1700s a Captain William Hollman, supported by Weymouth Corporation and local shipowners, petitioned Trinity House for a lighthouse on Portland Bill.

Trinity House is a national charity dedicated to safeguarding ships and their crews with a statutory responsibility as a General Lighthouse Authority to deliver reliable, efficient and cost-effective aid to navigation for all.

Despite the area's record for shipwrecks and navigational issues, Trinity House did not consider a lighthouse was required on Portland Bill. Local requests and demands continued until on 26 May 1716 King George I granted a patent to allow the erection of two lighthouses. A lease for sixty-one years was obtained and two coal-fired lighthouses were erected. Together these could be viewed in alignment by passing ships to guide them through the channel.

When inspected by Trinity House they were found to be poorly maintained and often not lit at suitable times. When the lease expired and reverted to Trinity House UK fresh plans were laid.

To mark the presence of the low shelf of Portland sandstone extending out from the headland, which was often under water, an obelisk was erected in 1844 and is still present today, standing some distance along the Bill from the main lighthouse.

In 1879 a new lighthouse was built by William Johns of Weymouth. It was repositioned to make it more visible during daylight, and in August 1788 was the first lighthouse in England to receive the new and more powerful Argand lamps, their greater power enhanced by a bank of lenses.

New lighthouses were built in 1896, and the current single structure designed by Sir Thoms Matthews was built and made operational in 1906. Construction was carried out by Wakeham Brothers of Plymouth. The move to a new, single lighthouse was driven by the growing importance of Portland as a naval base and an unusually high number of shipwrecks over the winter of 1901.

The lighthouse was fitted with the latest type of pressurised paraffin lamp supplied by Chance and Co. of Smethwick, Birmingham. With its revolving lenses the structure weighed 3.5 tons. A red sector light was also installed to shine from a lower window to show the location of the Shambles.

From 1940 a fog Diaphone Type F signal (or fog-horn to less nautical types) was installed part-way up the tower and sounded through a convenient window some 65 feet above the ground. When activated it would sound a 3.5-second blast every 30 seconds. This was usually audible up to 7 nautical miles away, but could be heard much further way under favourable weather conditions. It was replaced in 1995 by an electric fog-warning device operating from a lower window. Restored in 2003, the original audible fog-warning device is now occasionally sounded purely for the enjoyment of visitors to what is the Isle of Portland's foremost tourist attraction. For a time, it was sounded regularly every Sunday morning, as long as there was no actual fog.

By repute the job of a lighthouse keeper is one of the most boring and stressful there is, so it no doubt came as a relief when the Portland Bill Lighthouse was automated on 18 March 1996.

The old lighthouse keeper buildings were remodelled and opened to the public, displaying a history of the Portland Bill Lighthouse in March 2015. There are 153 steps from ground level to the magnificent views from the upper light room, and any visitor who manages them all is awarded a badge.

The lighthouse itself has been a listed building since May 1993, and the obelisk before it marking out the shallow water was listed in September 1978.

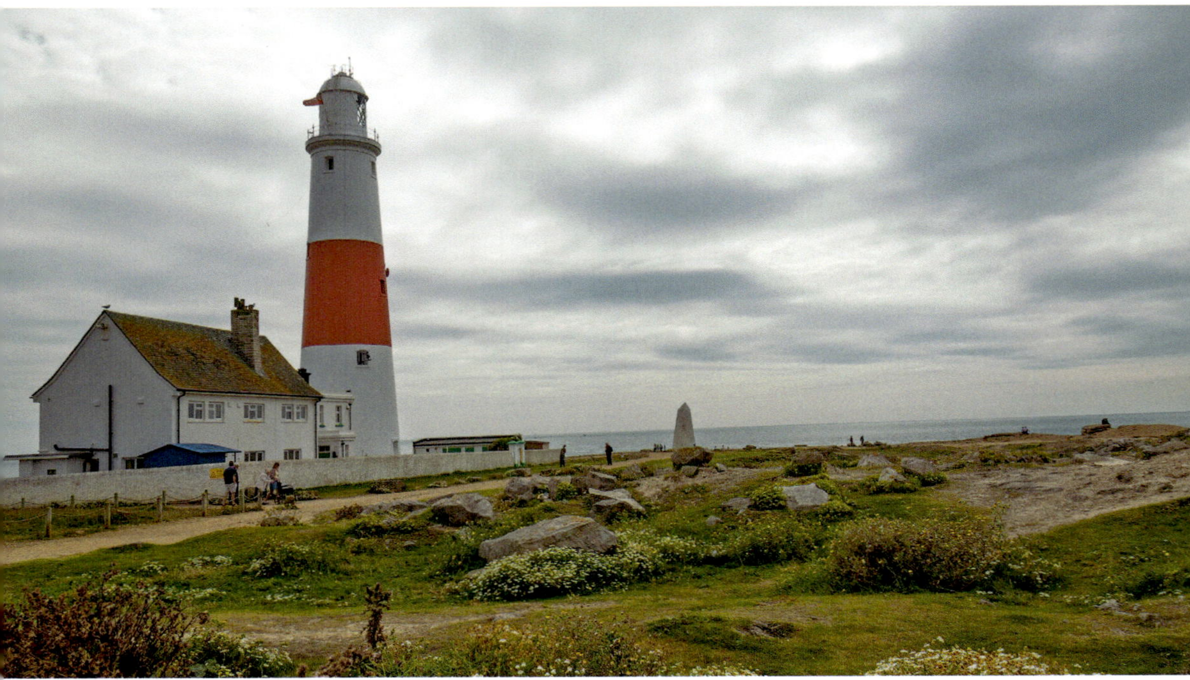

Portland Bill Lighthouse with obelisk showing the limit of the rock shelf in front.

M

Merchant Navy Memorial

The Esplanade in Weymouth may hold the record for the number of military memorials along its length.

At the very far end of the Esplanade, beyond the ANZAC memorial, is a relatively new memorial to the fallen of the Merchant Navy and fishing fleet lost during the both World Wars and subsequent conflicts.

Unveiled by Angus Campbell Esq., Lord Lieutenant of Dorset, on 9 November 2016 at the traditional time of 11 a.m., it is a structure of Portland stone weighing 5 tons. It is carved in the shape of the upturned bow of a sinking ship with bronze anchors mounted on the very front of the bow. A bronze plaque of the badge of the Merchant Navy is displayed on the top seaward-facing surface. Below this sits two large bronze plaques with dedications of remembrance and the crossed flags of the British ensign. A large casting of the coat of arms of the Merchant Navy is mounted on the rear/landward side of the memorial.

The memorial is surrounded by a low black railing that has coloured representations of the flags of the Merchant Navy and letters 'MN' cast into it.

Plans were laid for the memorial in 2010 when a Merchant Navy Association branch was founded in Weymouth and Portland. The design of the memorial was proposed and the plans created for it by David Kennet, a former Chief Engineer. Planning permission

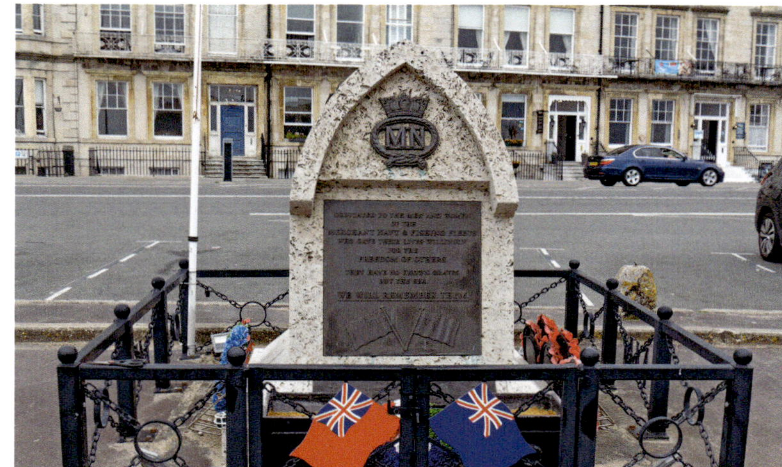

The Merchant Seamen memorial to those lost in combat.

was granted by the council without any objections as the memorial was considered fitting for a place such as Weymouth with its long connections with seafaring, and the £20,000 budget was raised remarkably quickly. With the aim of making the new memorial a very local production, the block of Portland stone was quarried from Portland, the bronze plaques cast locally in Bridport and the railings around the monument were manufactured in Weymouth itself. A fitting effort to keep all the production local as so much of the funds raised came from the immediate local area.

Mulberry Harbour

If you look beyond Portland harbour breakwater (or down on it from Portland) you will see two tall, square, concrete structures surrounded by the sea. These are two of the famous Mulberry harbour concrete Phoenix caissons created during the Second World War to allow the Allies to effectively take their own self-assembly harbour to Normandy to allow resupply following D-Day in June 1944.

These are two of the once ten such surplus caissons that were placed here in 1946 to protect the harbour and to allow mooring for the Royal Navy's latest Battle class destroyers. They also shielded the coastline while building work was ongoing to improve the harbour and the construction of the new Queens Pier.

Following catastrophic flooding in Holland in 1953 eight of the caissons were refloated and towed to Holland to repair holes in the Dykes. The last two caissons were moved to their current location opposite the Castletown Pier in 1962 to provide shelter to the harbour. Each required nearly 8,000 gallons of water to be pumped from them before they could be floated into their new position. Each caisson weighs around 7,000 tons empty and considerably more once flooded and seated securely on the seabed.

On 6 June 2017 six life-size sculptures of servicemen who would have used them during D-Day were unveiled on top of the caissons. They depict two Royal Navy sailors, two dock workers and two American soldiers.

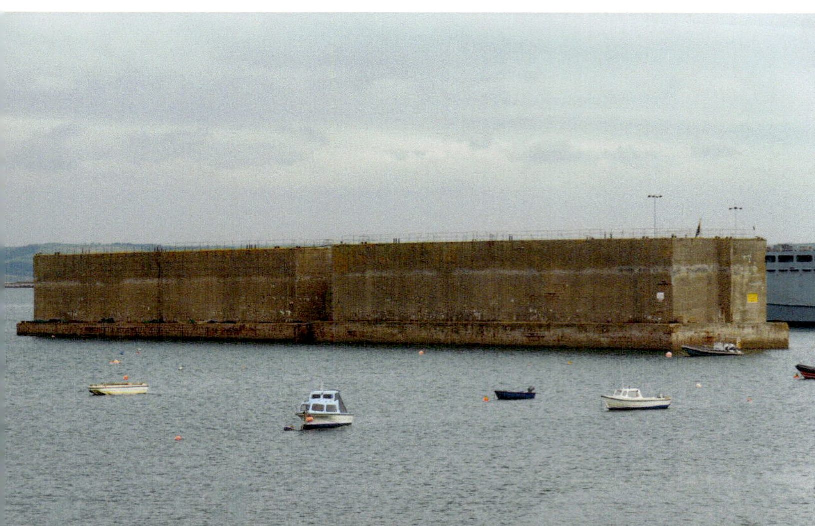

The Mulberry harbour section opposite Castletown Pier.

Nothe Fort

Nothe Fort dominates the skyline at the southern edge of the bay overlooking the harbour, sitting at the end of the predictably named Barrack Road beyond what is now known as Nothe Gardens and was originally just known as The Nothe.

Construction of the fort was started in 1859 and was originally part of a set of four designed to protect the harbour from the French fleet. The others were located on The Verne and the ends of the then newly constructed harbour breakwaters.

Construction of Nothe Fort itself was commenced in 1859 by fifty sappers of 26th Company The Royal Engineers under Captain P. Smith and Colonel J. Hirse, work being completed in 1869. It was designed to feature deep ammunition magazines and bomb-proof casemates to protect the guns.

As the wars with the French were long over by then, the fort was not actually armed until 1872 when a dozen 10-inch-calibre muzzle-loaded coastal defence guns were installed in the casemates around the outer edge of the fort covering the approaches to the harbour from all directions. They would be joined by a pair of large 64-pounders and four 9-inch-calibre rifled muzzle loaders.

In 1892 seven of the 10-inch guns were replaced by newer 12.5-inch rifled muzzle-loading guns which offered a huge improvement in range and accuracy of Nothe Fort's armaments.

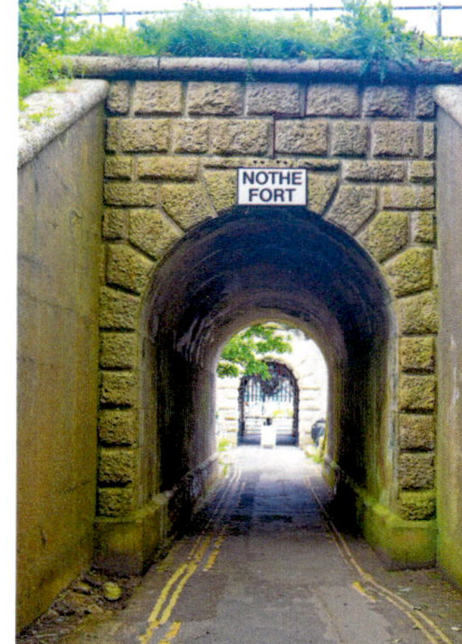

The narrow entrance to Nothe Fort from Nothe Gardens.

The now vintage muzzle loaders were replaced in 1903 by a pair of 6-inch-calibre breech-loading guns on the ramparts to allow a smaller number of guns to cover the same field of fire as the previous larger number. They were capable of firing both faster, further and more accurately than their predecessors. A third gun would be added in 1908.

With the imminent risk of invasion, fading Nothe Fort was decommissioned as a gun platform after the First World War.

During Second World War Nothe Fort had two of the 6-inch guns recommissioned for defence of the harbour and the American units preparing for the Normandy landings in 1944. From 1938 the huge and well-protected ammunition magazines from the fort's early days were utilised for storage and distribution of anti-aircraft ammunition for the whole of the South West.

Light anti-aircraft guns were added to the fort itself (one remains on the front rampart where its traverse mechanism still operates to the delight of generations of visiting children and no small number of visiting adults), while heavy anti-aircraft guns were placed in what is now the car park where they could fire in defence of both the town and the harbour.

Nothe Fort remained in service until the dissolution of the UK's coastal defence programme in 1956. Used afterwards for general military storage by the Royal Navy, it would eventually be purchased by the council in 1961 and be allowed to fall into disrepair.

Grand plans to turn the now largely derelict fort into a luxury hotel were started and sadly abandoned in the early 1970s.

Briefly, at the height of the Cold War a deep part of the old ammunition magazines would find itself repurposed as a Civil Defence Nuclear Bunker. In the event of a nuclear attack this would have become a local civil administration centre with accommodation for around thirty staff. A heavy door was installed to resist an atomic blast before the bunker was decommissioned, thankfully unused, in 1990.

Notional Lottery and English Heritage grants have allowed a team of nearly 100 volunteers to restore large parts of the fort, opening it to the public in 1980 and remaining open to this day. The local council website cheerfully describes it as Weymouth's 'foremost heritage visitor attraction'. The fort itself was made a listed

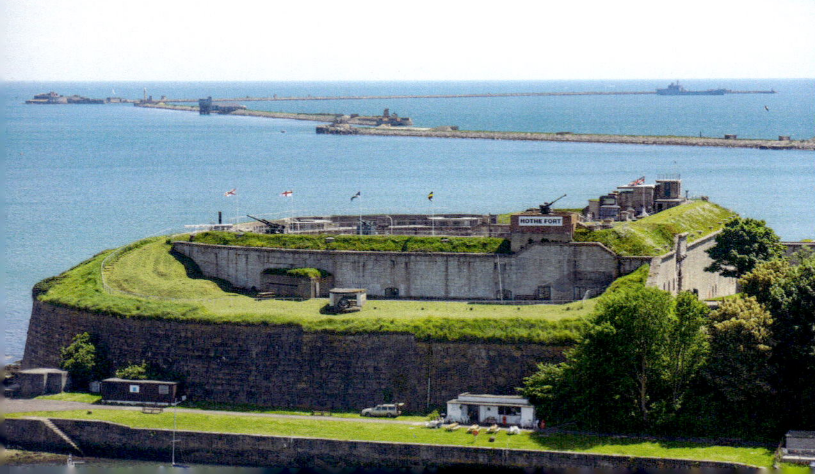

Nothe Fort.

building in 1974 and its associated Fusee steps (which have their own entry) were listed in 2000.

In 2007 a National Lottery survey found Nothe Fort voted as one of the spookiest tourist locations in the UK, and every other weekend you can hear the boom of cannon and fire and the occasional crackle of musketry as the volunteers, in their remarkably accurate period uniforms, demonstrate weapons from the fort's past.

In 2024 Nothe Fort was named England's best small visitor attraction by VisitEngland.

Nothe Gardens

While Nothe headland will always be best known for Nothe Fort at its seaward end the ornamental gardens surrounding it are worthy of examination in their own right. Laid out in an informal manner, the gardens offer wonderful views out over Portland harbour and Portland itself beyond. During the 2012 Olympics the gardens were a much-favoured location to watch the sailing events below and the council found it necessary to organise a ticketing system to prevent dangerous overcrowding in the gardens.

The area that is now Nothe Gardens was first formally organised as a military encampment and the gardens as they are now were begun in 1888. Over the years a wide network of pathways was created and the gardens became a haven for wildlife. Currently visitors can expect to see many grey squirrels in the trees, slow worms, roe deer, badgers and foxes, among others. There is a formal nature trail with a freely available map of the eight points spread over the gardens to entertain the young and young at heart, as well as an orienteering path for the more energetic visitor. And for the extremely energetic the South West Coast Path runs through the gardens as a tiny part of its 630-mile length that runs from an incredible sculpture in Minehead in north Somerset to Poole in Dorset.

The gardens are now looked after by a group of locally recruited volunteers named 'Friends of Nothe Gardens' whose stated aim is to make Nothe Gardens 'a jewel amongst Weymouth's attractions'.

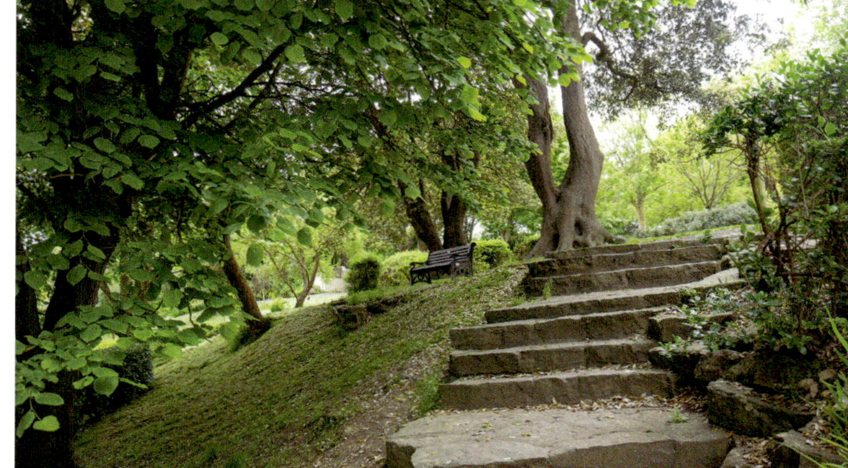

Nothe Gardens offer a maze of walks, seating and a curated green space.

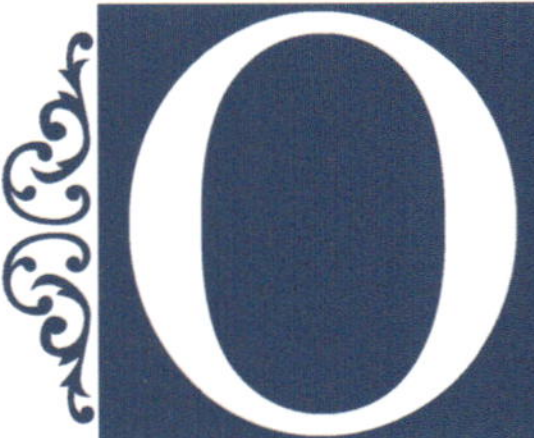

Old Customs House

On the north side of the harbour, if you look up as you pass what at first looks like a plain red-brick building, you will see a magnificent coat of arms above a very striking door. This building is the Old Customs House which gives its name to this stretch of the walkway that adjoins the harbour, Customs House Quay.

Originally built as a warehouse and home in 1794, it was operated by Messrs Robilliard and Ahier as a business premise. Later owner Sir Frederick Johnstone leased it to HM Customs service in 1794 and it continued in their use as a customs house until 1985.

Portland's HM Coastguard took over the property and in 1988 opened it as a maritime rescue sub-centre, a function it continued to carry out until September 2014 when the centre was closed down and the building sold as part of government cuts.

The building was refurbished in civilian life and now houses residential properties and a café on the ground floor.

As with many of the older buildings surrounding the harbour in Weymouth, the Old Customs House has been listed since 1970.

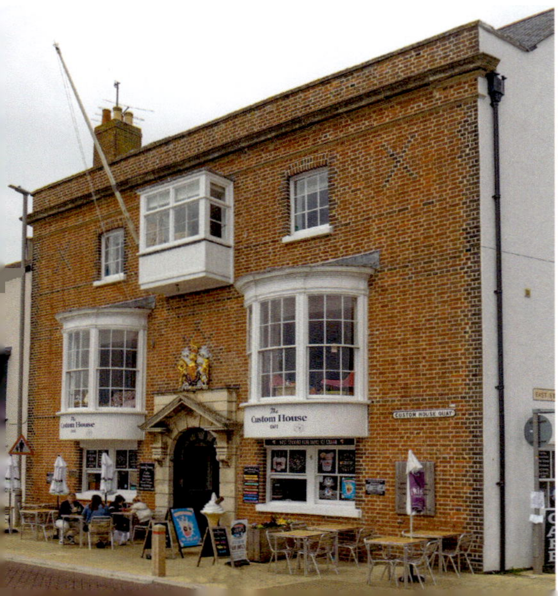

The Old Customs House on Custom House Quay.

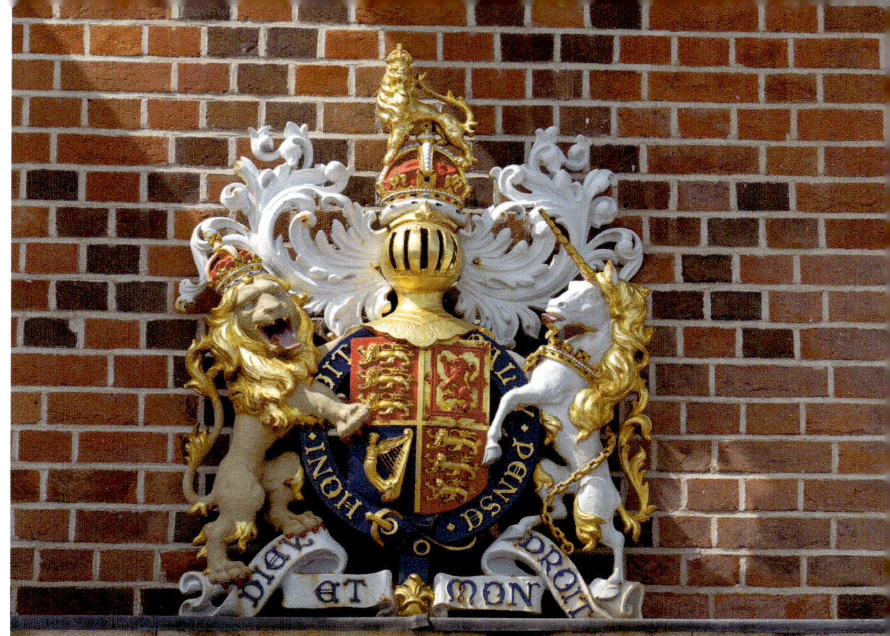

The coat of arms that remains over the door on the Old Customs House café.

Old Fish Market

Facing out onto the quayside of the harbour is the Weyfish restaurant. Built of the distinctive local Portland stone with tall arched windows and doorway, the architecture stands out from the adjoining much younger buildings. This is not surprising as the restaurant building was once the harbour fish market.

Built in 1885 to a plan by British architect Thomas Talbot Bury (who had been apprenticed to no less a luminary than Augustus Pugin before starting his own design business), it was constructed to offer a permanent home to the twice-weekly fish markets where the local fishing fleet landed their catches in the quay right outside the doors. The original building was built to include an ice room for the preservation of the fish before they were sent to other parts of the UK.

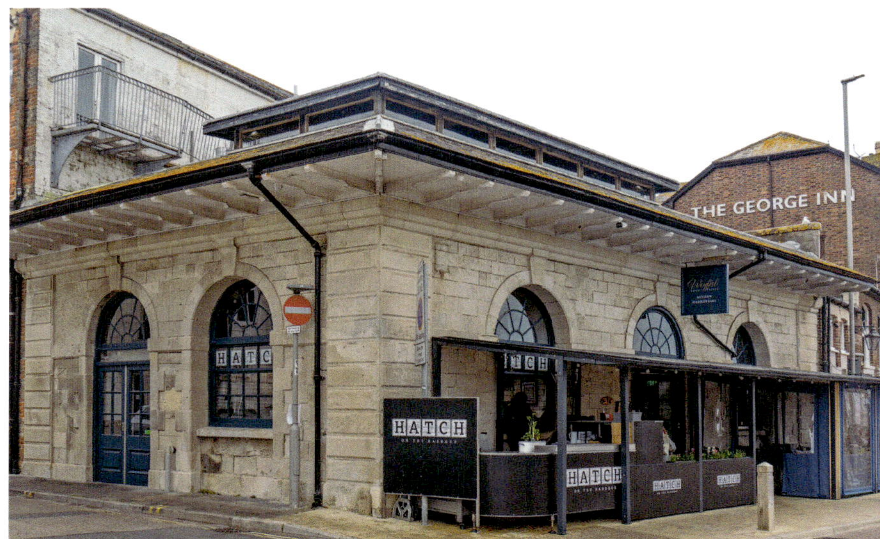

The now repurposed old fish market.

Sadly, the original use ended not long after the fine building was constructed (some say after as few as fifteen years) when the unloading of coal on the adjoining quayside caused the coal dust to contaminate the fish. For many years it was used for the storage of other materials being offloaded from boats including coal and fertiliser before falling into disrepair. It was restored in 1988 to the original use as a fish market for locally caught fish and a supporting restaurant.

Osmington White Horse

If you look north along the Esplanade to the hills beyond, or even better north from the elevated platform that is Nothe Fort, you will see on the side of the grassy hills facing you the outline of a figure on horseback carved into the limestone of Osmington Hill. This is the Osmington White Horse.

The hill figure was created in 1808 and depicts King George III riding his favourite grey charger, Adonis. It was created as a tribute to the King after his patronage made Weymouth nationally famous. And it is visible from literally miles around and from out to sea. At one point Admiralty charts listed it as a 'seamark' which could be used by passing ships for navigation.

The figure is 208 feet high and 323 feet long. It is considered unique in that the carving depicts both a person and a horse together in a single hill figure – many others are one or the other, but no others have both. The figure was created under the auspices of John Ranier, who financed the creation; James Hamilton, a local architect who was also involved with the design of the King's statue in the middle of Weymouth; local landowner Robert Wood; and Weymouth bookseller John Wood.

Legend has it that the King was offended when he saw that he was depicted riding away from Weymouth rather than towards it and never returned to the town again.

The figure has been rather neglected at various times over the years and it has been tidied up by the Scouts, television's Anneka Rice, and during the First World War by

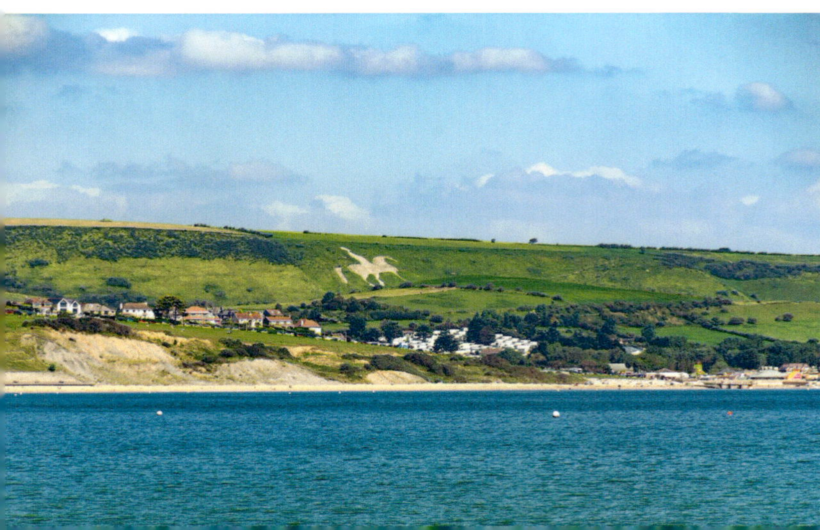

The Osmington White Horse.

bored and presumably convalescing Australian soldiers. The figure was restored and recut again in time for the 2012 Olympics, Princess Anne unveiling a plaque made of locally sourced stone on 11 March 2012.

The figure is officially listed as a Scheduled Monument under the Ancient Monuments and Archaeological Areas Act, and was at one time prior to the restoration listed as a Monument at Risk.

The White Horse had a brief moment of fame in August 2011 when persons unknown added a unicorn horn fabricated from plastic sheet to the figure, which was swiftly removed.

Olympic Rings

Weighing in at 9 tonnes and standing 3.8 metres long by 2.5 metres tall, the sculpture of the Olympic rings stands on Portland Heights on the Isle of Portland. Created from ten separate pieces of stone joined by steel rods, it dates from 2012 when Weymouth hosted the sailing portion of the Olympic Games in the UK.

Created locally at the Albion stone workshops on Portland itself from the local Portland stone, the rings originally stood outside the railway station for the duration of the Olympics before being placed at their current location as a stunning addition to the viewpoint and a reminder of the time Weymouth was in the view of the whole world.

Never intended as anything other than a standing sculpture, when people started climbing on the rings there were well-publicised fears of them falling, one report using the notable understatement that they would 'do serious harm if to they were to fall on someone'. Thankfully this nightmare scenario never occurred and the rings still stand today calling attention to the glorious view of Portland harbour and the sailing academy behind them.

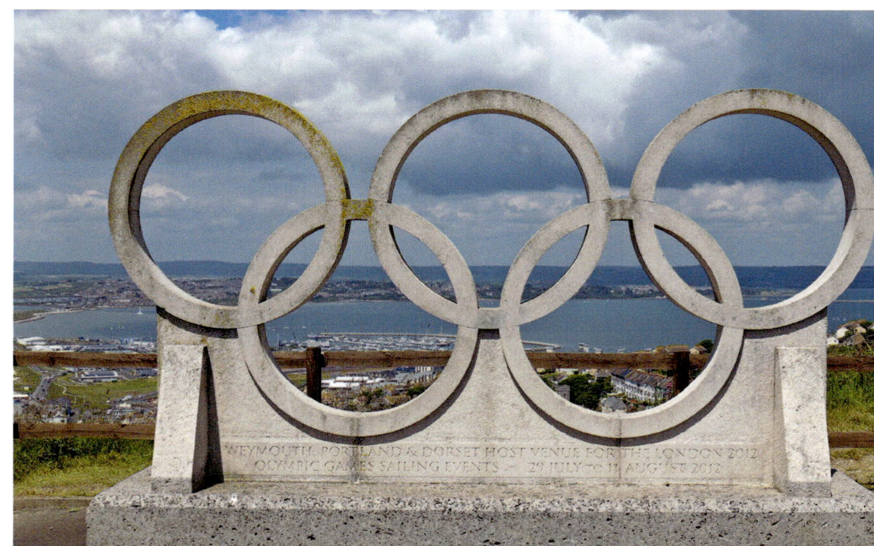

The Olympic rings looking down on Weymouth from Portland Heights.

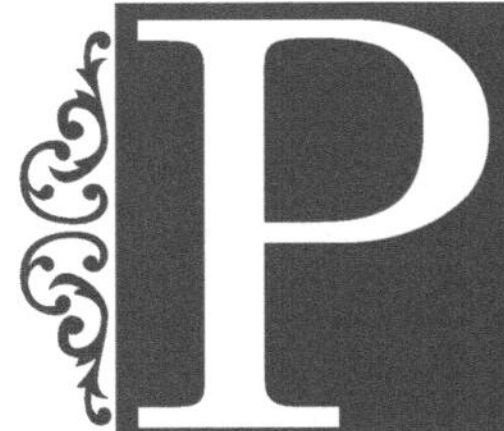

Pavilion

The Weymouth Pavilion entertainment venue at the far southern end of the Esplanade was originally opened in 1907 and remains Weymouth's foremost mass entertainment venue. The venue was originally financed by the local council in the face of considerable opposition from the local taxpayers' associations.

Initially built as a wooden structure over a steel frame on what was then known as the Pile Pier, it was opened on 21 December 1908 by the Earl and Countess of Shaftesbury. The owners had arranged for a special train to bring journalists from London to cover the event in the metropolitan newspapers.

A handsome building with an entrance flanked by two towers, it was built in response to Weymouth's rapid growth as a tourist resort with the arrival of regular railway services. Two days after the official opening the first performance took place, the Christmas pantomime *Mother Goose*.

To save local taxpayers money from 1914 the local council leased its operation to Ernest Wheeler, a member of a prominent local family of businessmen who already had entertainment interests in Weymouth. He would continue to run it for a quarter of a century. From 1925, in response to competition from the new Alexandra Garden Theatre the Pavilion started to screen films.

During the dark days of the Second World War the Pavilion was taken over by the military. At various times it was occupied by No. 4 Commando, provided a home for hundreds of Moroccan soldiers from the French army, as a hospital and finally as an Admiralty postal sorting office before being handed back into civilian hands in 1947. The military services had not been kind to the building and in common with many local authorities the council had a long fight to get compensation to return the building to a useable state.

The theatre was refitted in 1950 under the Buxton Theatres group and was reopened as The Ritz.

During restoration work in 1954 a fire on 13 April caused by the improper use of a blow lamp on the old timber over steel building led to a fire. As the building was largely made up of old, dried-out timber, it – according to reports of the time – it burned to the ground in less than an hour. The site was cleared and plans laid for a new building.

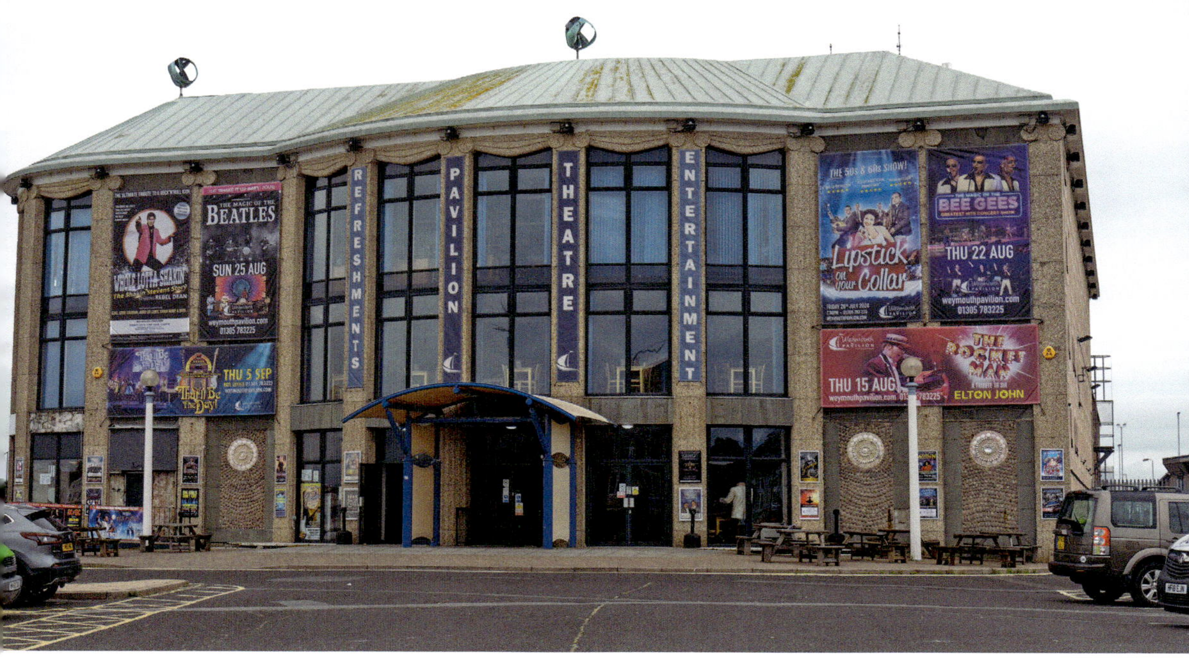

Weymouth Pavilion at the southern end of the Esplanade.

The construction of the building you see today was started in September 1958 to a design by Samuel Beverley. A local newspaper ran a competition to name the new venue in 1959 and the winner was to return to the original name of The Pavilion, with the name The Normandy in second place. The old name of The Ritz would rise again and be used as the name of the restaurant in the venue today.

The new venue was officially opened on 15 July 1960 to a performance of *Let's Make a Night of It* starring Benny Hill.

Ongoing plans to redevelop the ageing building complex in the early years of the twenty-first century came to nothing despite the forecast arrival of the Olympics in Weymouth in 2012. Serious consideration was given to demolishing the Pavilion by the council. In the face of a local petition control of the venue passed into the hands of a community interest company who intended to run it as a non-profit organisation, all organised by local businessman Phil Say. The Pavilion finally opened under this new management on Saturday 13 July 2013 and as of the time of writing is still going strong.

Pier Bandstand

At the far northern end of the Esplanade you will find a delightful art deco building proclaiming 'The Pier Bandstand', the title being split by a square clock and surmounted by a line of three Union Jack flags. But beyond the building there is nothing to be seen, no pier for the bandstand to belong to.

The current building is all that remains of what was once a much larger pier extending out into Weymouth Bay. It was built in 1938 to a design by V. B. J. Venning

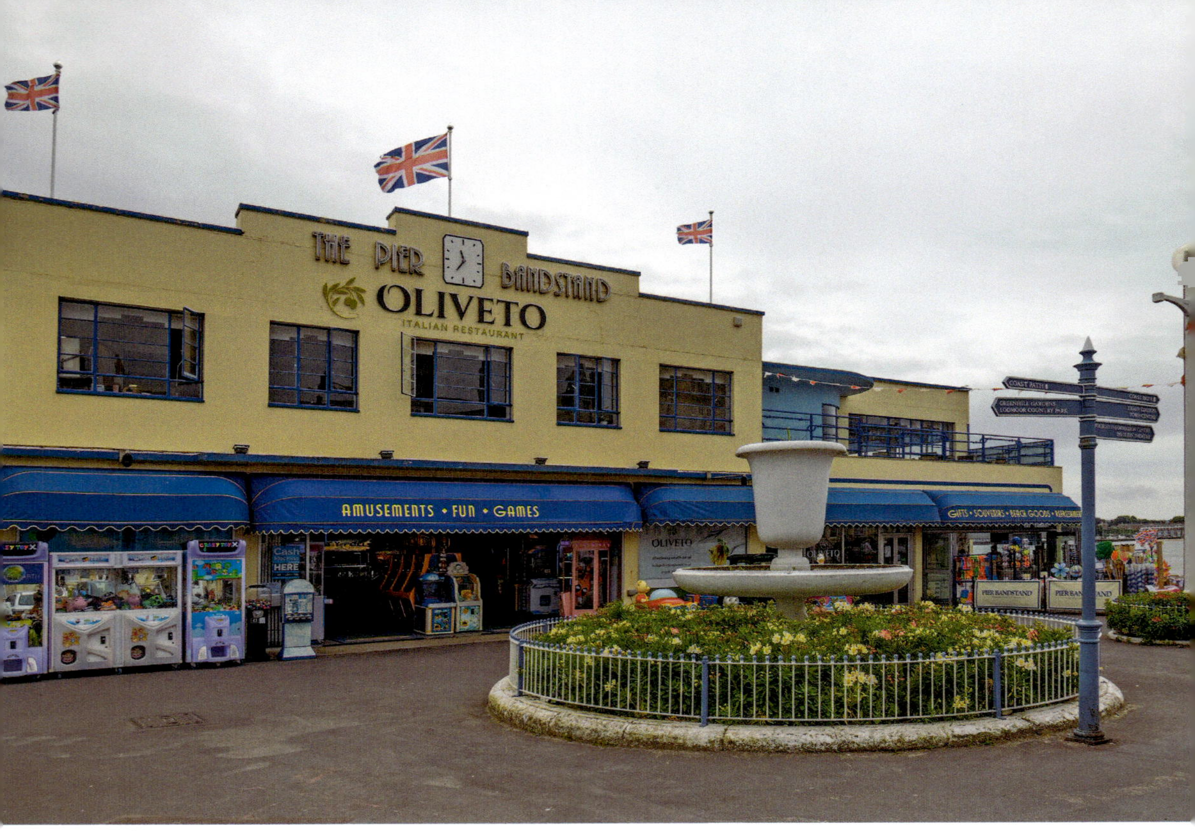

The landward remains of the Pier Bandstand.

who won a design competition of twenty-six entries overseen by the Royal Institute of British Architects. Construction was handled by local builder Christiani Neilson and the pier was opened on 25 May 1939 by Mayor of Weymouth J. T. Goddard.

Also dating from that time is the line of period lamp standards outside with their wide arms and the brightly planted three-level flower bed with the huge urn at its centre. At the height of the season there are bright flowers in the floor-level bed, the saucer section below the urn and a tiny display in the urn itself.

The structure was originally a bandstand at the level of the upper floor of the current building extending out from the remaining building into Weymouth Bay with an art deco stage at the seaward end. It was capable of seating 2,400 people with 800 of them under cover as the centre of the performance area was not covered. When performances were not taking place, amusement rides stood in the wide, flat central area, and people could eat on the pier at Pullinger's restaurant. At the far seaward end changing rooms were added for those brave enough to dive from the pier into Weymouth Bay.

A popular attraction in its day, the pier bandstand would over the years host musical performances, dances, sporting events and the annual Miss Weymouth bathing beauty competitions. Military bands in barracks locally were regular performers at the pier bandstand, as, much later, were pop groups. It was even possible to hire the pier as a wedding reception venue.

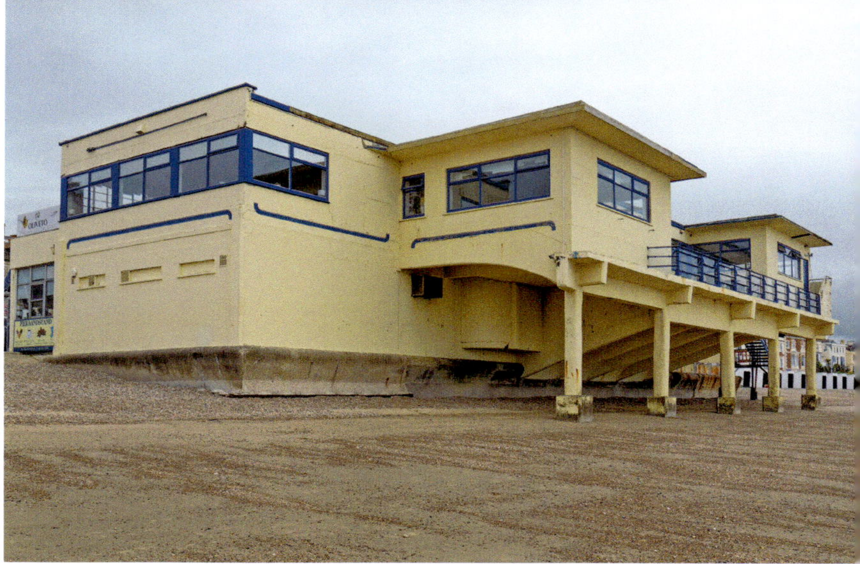

The seaward side of the Pier Bandstand showing where the previous pier once stood.

By the early 1980s the pier bandstand was starting to show its age and was considered in need of urgent repair work to ensure the safety of users. Faced with a £300,000 bill for repair or a £30,000 bill for demolition, Weymouth Council opted for the latter. On 4 May 1986 thousands of local people gathered on the Esplanade to witness the two Birmingham schoolgirls Carol and Susan Firth, who had won a national competition for the privilege, press the button to blow up the seaward end of the pier bandstand, leaving only what you see today remaining.

Plans to refurbish the landward building, create an art deco-style square on the Esplanade and reinstate the pier portion in time for the 2012 Olympics collapsed following a withdrawal of government funding.

Pier Memorials

Standing in front of the Pavilion at the southern end of the Esplanade is a monument that tells of Weymouth's involvement with the settlement of what was then referred to as the 'New World'.

Erected in 1914 and paid for by public subscription, the circular bronze plaque on a Portland stone column is enclosed by a floral wreath design and celebrates the achievements of Richard Clark, described as a 'Captain and Pilot of Weymouth', who joined Sir Humphrey Gilberts on the voyage that discovered Newfoundland in 1583.

Also commemorated is the voyage of John Endicott who set sail from Weymouth on the ship *Abigail* on 20 June 1628 on a voyage that led to the foundation of the colony of Salem (first called Naumkeag), Massachusetts, on land purchased from the Plymouth Company. He would become the Governor of the New England colony following the death of the incumbent Governor Winthrop on several occasions until his own death in 1665, and established their first mint.

The memorial was originally unveiled in 1914 by Mrs Joseph Chamberlain, a direct descendant of John Endicott.

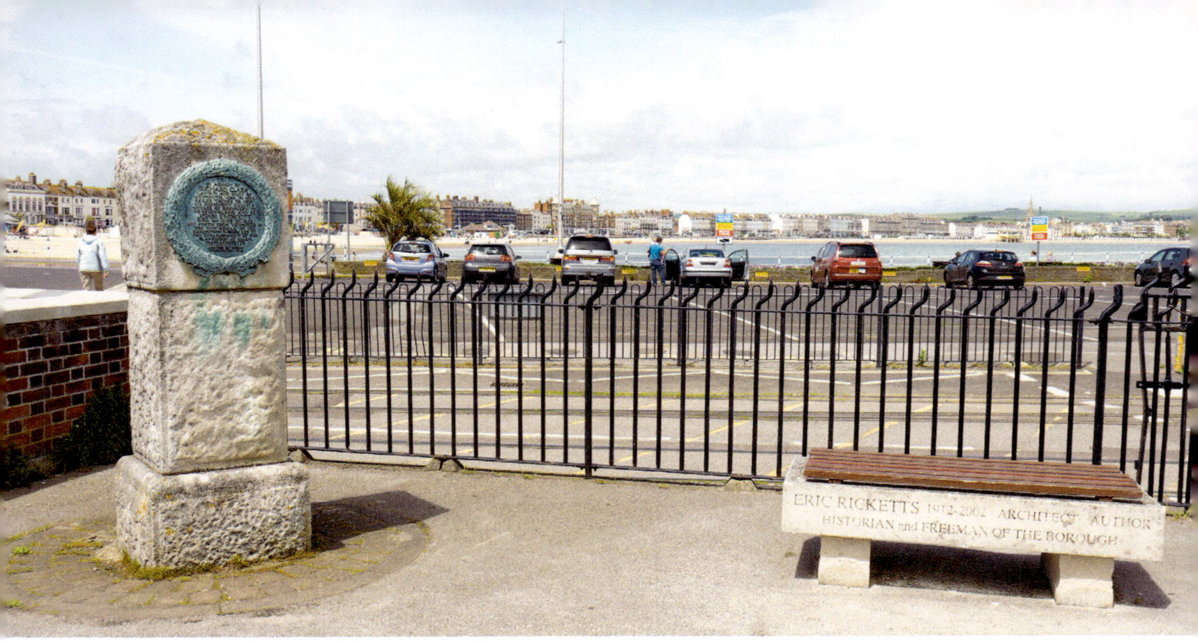

The pier memorials.

   The memorial was originally placed by the Pavilion, but following the fire that destroyed the Pavilion (or The Ritz as it was known then) the memorial spent some time in Alexandra Gardens before returning to this location in 1999, where overlooking the harbour was considered a far more fitting location for a memorial to such seafaring men.

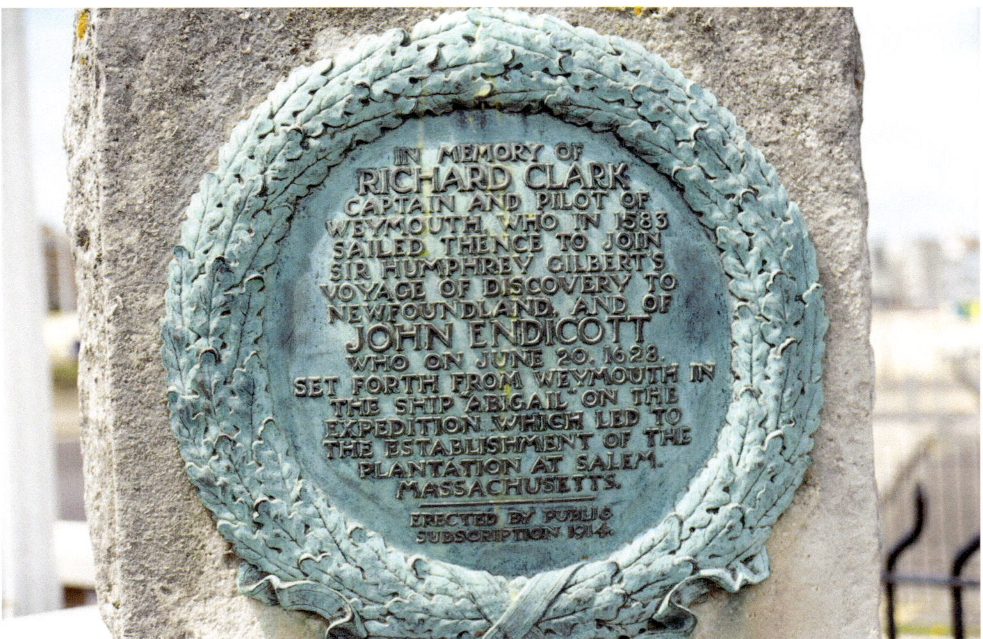

The pier memorial to Richard Clark and John Endicott unveiled in 1914.

It has been joined much more recently by a simple Portland stone memorial in the form of a bench dedicated by inscription to Eric Ricketts, local architect, author, historian and Freeman of the Borough. He is most famous for a set of four books he wrote describing the buildings of old Weymouth and Portland. His career as the assistant Dorset county architect influenced the look of several local buildings, most notably the Town Hall.

Plague

One of Weymouth's claims to fame for want of a better phrase is that it was the place the Plague or Black Death entered England. Popular local legend is that it came ashore at Custom House Quay at the junction with St Mary Street.

The first recorded instance of the Plague in England was 25 June 1348, brought ashore by a seaman on a ship landing at Melcombe Regis from Gascony. The arrival was documented precisely by the Grey friars' chronicle as being 'shortly before the feast of St John the Baptist' and described as bringing the 'seeds of that terrible pestilence'.

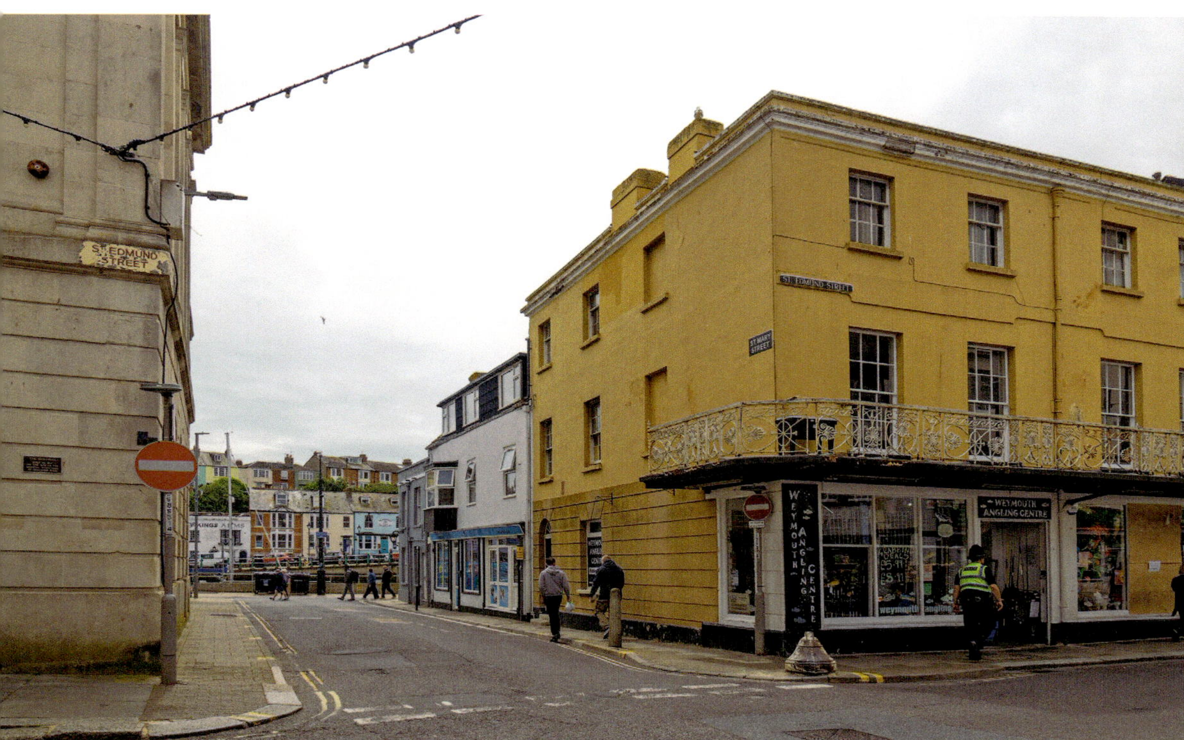

St Mary Street is, according to local legend, the place the Plague first arrived in England.

Already endemic on mainland Europe, the Plague had reached London by the autumn and was to be found over the entire country by the summer of 1349. Depending on which figures are considered correct, the Plague would lead to the deaths of between a third and a half of the population. In England it would start dying down by December 1349, and the last official case was recorded in 1679.

Portland Castle

Approached along the aptly named Mulberry Road and hiding behind a fancifully crenelated wall you will find Portland Castle, part of King Henry VIII's programme of fort building to protect southern England from invasion from Europe following his breaking away from the Catholic Church and forming the Church of England.

After this act Pope Paul III urged Charles V of the Holy Roman Empire and King Francis of France to unite and attack England. In February 1539 the 'Device of the King' was enacted and experts were despatched to recommend defensive measures for the south coast and Wales. Sir John Russell reported that the Portland Roads was a vital and sheltered deep-water harbour that should be protected.

As a result two forts were built to protect the harbour. One of these was Portland Castle. Conceived as a gun fort facing out towards the water of the harbour and the incoming fire it might receive, the outer walls of Portland Castle are curved to deflect incoming enemy fire, while the internal room is octagonal in shape. Constructed from the local Portland stone, the gun casemates point outwards towards the harbour in a fan-like configuration as each exits at a different point of the circle.

There are two levels of guns facing out to sea protected by stone casemates, with a third level of guns mounted atop the roof to further increase the available firepower. In 1547 the castle was well armed with fifteen guns including four large cannon designed for long-range action.

Castles of this time were traditionally only manned by a small garrison to carry out basic service duties, intending to be reinforced should the time for battle ever arrive. The first commander of Portland Castle was Carew Ralegh who commanded a unit of only eighteen men.

As was so often the case during times of peace, the once mighty castle was neglected and when Captain John Leweston arrived in 1574 he reported that none of the guns were fit for active service.

Following a similar report in 1623, repairs were made and by the time of the English Civil War and the arrival of a Royalist garrison all was reported to be in good order and the sizeable garrison extended the landward defences with earthworks lying well beyond the current boundaries.

Portland Castle fell to the forces of Parliament in 1642, was recaptured by Royalists in 1643, was subjected to a four-month siege in 1644, and another in 1646. Following the Battle of Weymouth, Portland Castle found itself isolated and following negotiations

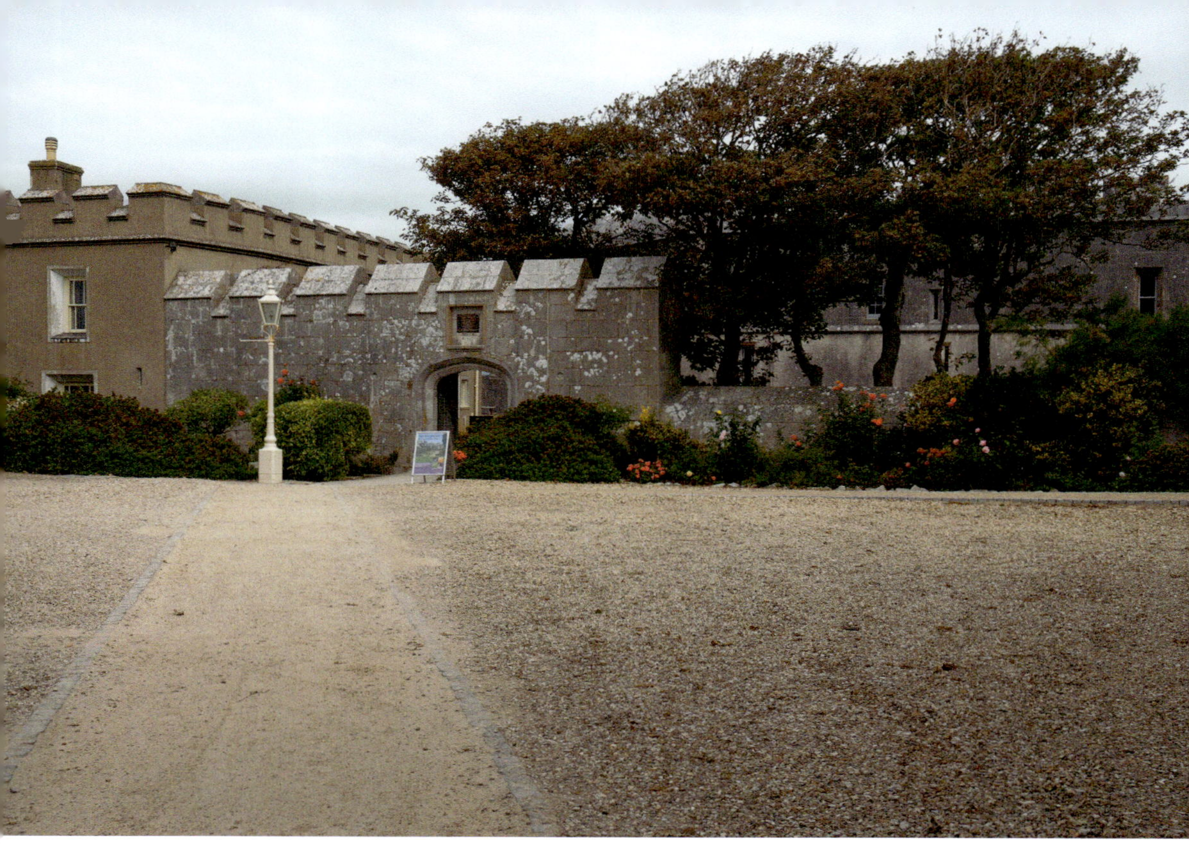

Portland Castle on the approach to the Isle of Portland.

the garrison surrendered to Vice Admiral William Batten and was permitted to leave unharmed.

After the Restoration of the Monarchy in the form of King Charles II the castle was restored and extended, mounting sixteen large guns in the original building and ten more on two new gun platforms on either side.

Following another lengthy period of neglect, in 1816 the largely derelict castle was leased to the Reverend John Manning, a Portland churchman who developed the building as a family residence and whose input to the styling of the building is today visible in the Captain's House and who laid out the gardens still visible today.

During the First World War Portland Castle was a base for Royal Navy seaplanes hunting German U-boats in the English Channel. Royal Air Force took this over from 1918 to 1919, the Royal Navy returned in the form of HMS Osprey anti-submarine warfare training unit from 1920 to 1980, and the Captain's House remained the residence of the Commanding Officer of HMS Osprey until 1999.

From 1955 ever-increasing parts of the castle were opened to the public, the government's Ministry of Works deciding to present the castle as it would have looked in the sixteenth century and many of the additions made by the Manning family were removed. Today Portland Castle is a listed building (since 1993) and English Heritage keep the site well maintained for visitors. It remains one of the finest preserved of all England's Tudor forts.

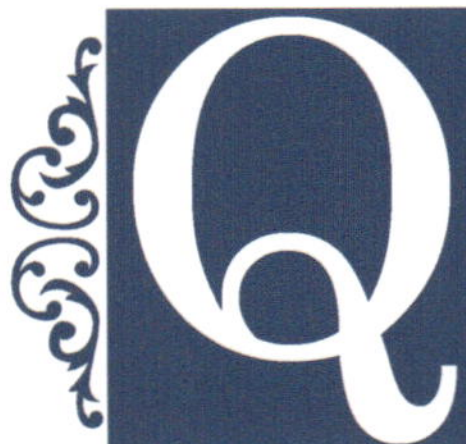

Queen Victoria

At the very northern end of the seafront where Dorchester Road swings inland, on a triangular traffic island stands a larger-than-life-sized bronze statue of Queen Victoria mounted on a 2-metre-high plinth of the traditional local Portland stone with bronze dolphins at the base. The statue looks proudly out along the Esplanade and over Weymouth Bay with the Church of St John to her back. Historic England describe the location as being in a 'good position at the north entry to the town, but is less favourably placed than the corresponding statue at the south end of the Esplanade', referring to that of King George III.

The podium upon which she stands has four faces. One has the royal coat of arms carved into it, the opposite face bearing the coat of arms of the Borough of Melcombe Regis. The other panels detail the history and background of the statue.

Erected using funds collected through public subscription by the Mayor of Weymouth John Bagg, it was unveiled to celebrate the reign of Queen Victoria on 20 October 1902 by no lesser a dignitary than Princess Beatrice (officially known as Princess Henry) of Battenberg.

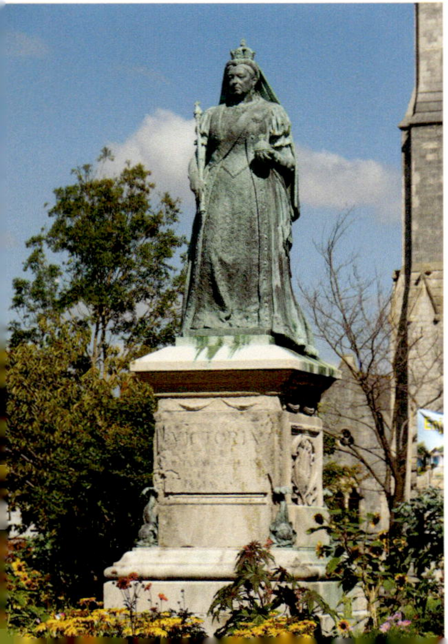

The statue of Queen Victoria stands on Dorchester Road.

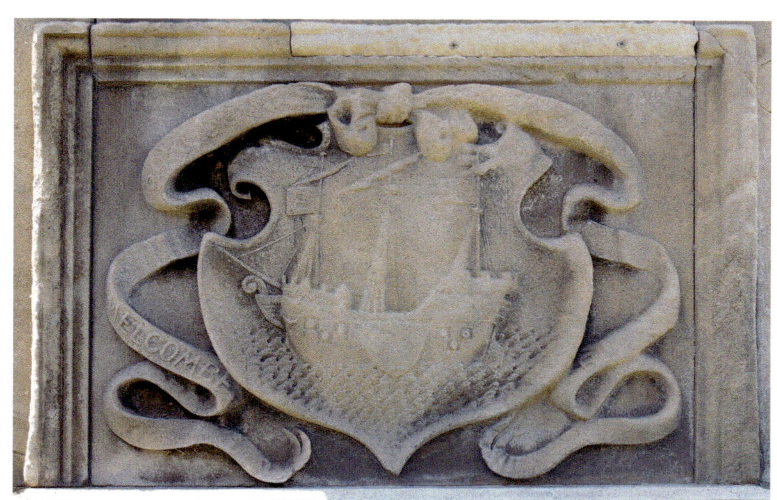

The worn Melcombe Regis coat of arms on the Queen Victoria statue.

The statue was designed by George Blackall Simonds using studies he made of Queen Victoria for a statue in Reading, reused here as they had already been granted royal approval. Both the royal orb and sceptre are remarkably detailed in their casting. The statue was cast by Singers of Frome.

It was given listed status in 1997 and was thoroughly cleaned in 2009 in preparation for the anticipated crowds of the 2012 Olympics.

Queen Victoria's Golden Jubilee is also celebrated in a more modest manner by a colourful slightly larger-than life-sized bust on Weymouth Bay facing the frontage of the Fairhaven Hotel (formerly the Victoria Hotel) at the opposite end of the Esplanade. In a moment of careful thought sufficient space was left on the mounting of the bust to add the year of her Diamond Jubilee ten years later.

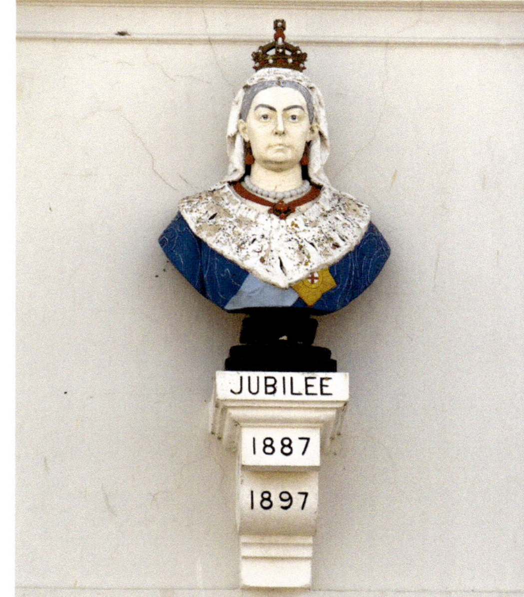

The Queen Victoria Jubilee bust on the Fairhaven (formerly the Victoria) Hotel.

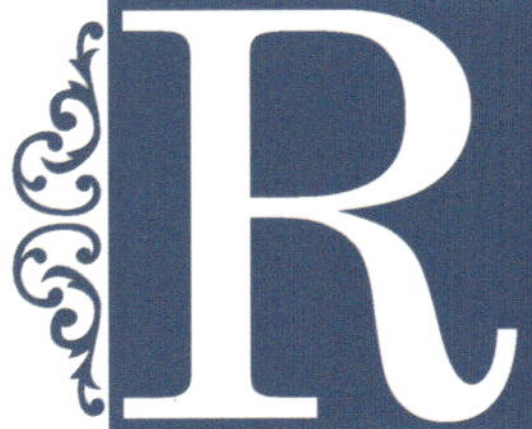

Radipole Lake

Clearly visible on your left as you approach Weymouth by car, Radipole Lake is an RSPB-managed wildlife sanctuary in what was originally the estuary of the River Wey (which gives the town of Weymouth its name). It is considered an important habitat for reed bed nesting birds and is watched over by the thatched RSPB discovery centre in a corner of the huge Swannery car park.

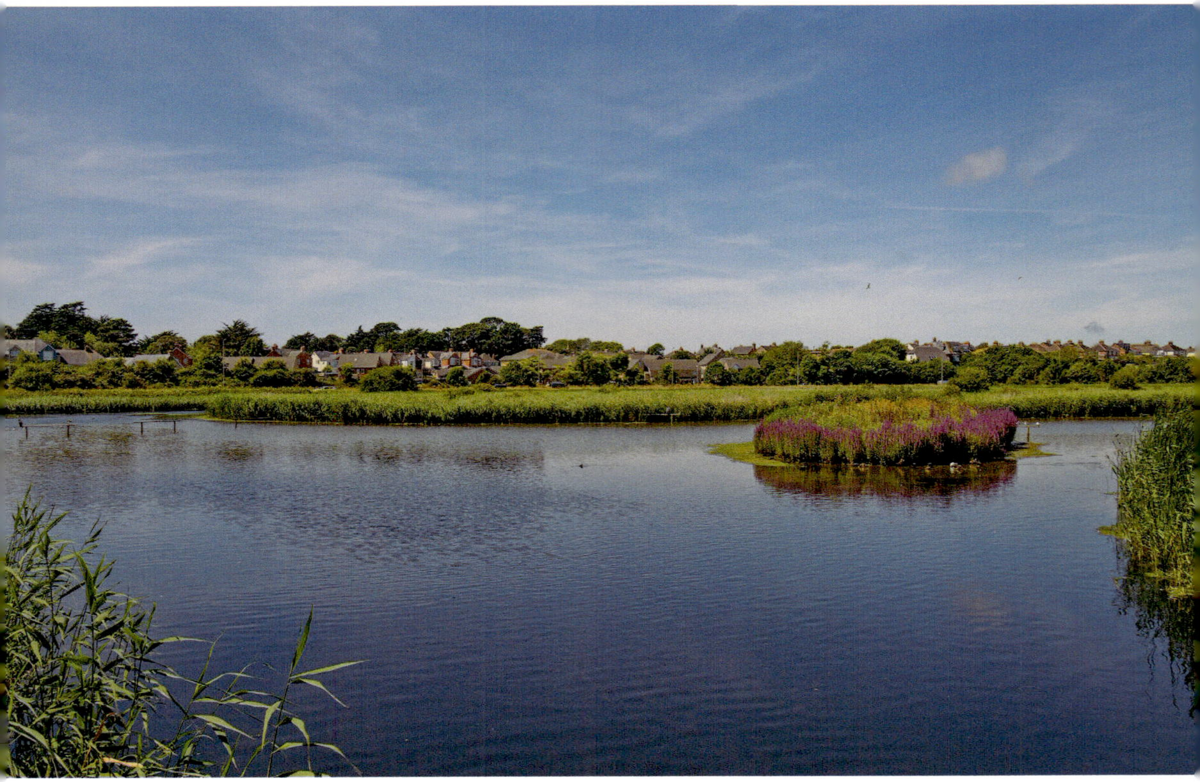

The RSPB-managed Radipole Lake.

Despite being managed by the RSPB, the range of wildlife to been seen around the lake is not entirely avian. Alongside the kingfishers, swallows, dunlins, snipe and lapwings there are otters and water voles. There are many footpaths to take visitors out among the reed beds and small lagoons to view the wildlife at close quarters.

Covering some 83 hectares, Radipole Lake is designated as an area of Special Scientific Interest. Numerous archaeological finds around the borders of the lake suggest human activity in the area was taking place as far back as Ancient times, and there is a popular local opinion that Radipole was once the Roman port of Clavinium from which a road led to the Roman town of Durnovaria, or modern-day Dorchester.

To create more building land for Weymouth, reclamation of the estuary began as early as the visits of King George III and slowly but surely the tidal estuary was reduced and moved further inland until the landscape you see today was created. For many years the resulting lake was known as 'Backwater' (as opposed to the front water of the seafront) and only in Victorian times did it get rechristened Radipole Lake in an attempt to make it sound more attractive.

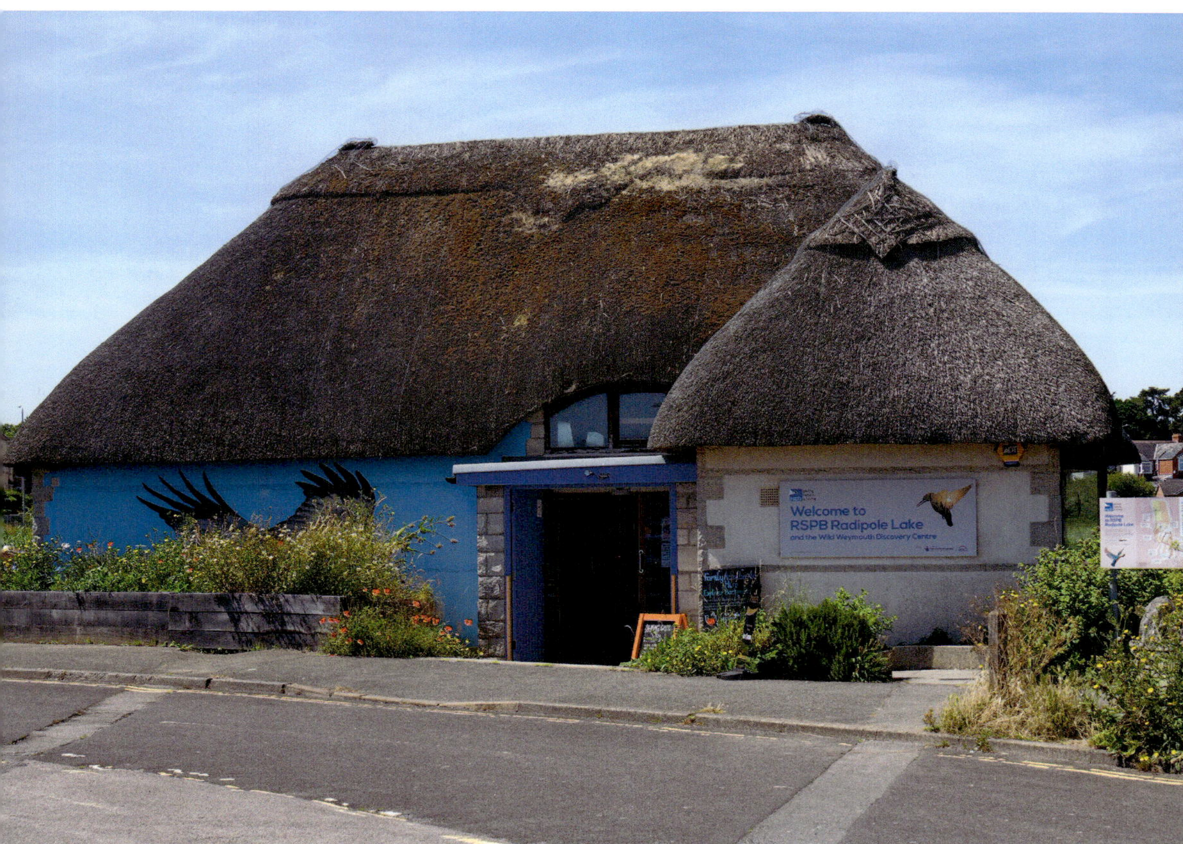

The thatched RSPB centre at Radipole Lake.

The swans now present at Radipole Lake were initially supplied by the Earl of Ilchester who owned nearby Abbotsbury Swannery in 1859. A popular tourist attraction in their own right, culls were carried out for food during both World Wars before the remaining swans were set free to roam the reed beds of the lake as they wished, and they can still be seen happily roosting there today.

Rangers Way

Immediately to the south side of Greenhill Gardens is a rough set of steps leading down to the coast. These were constructed in 1944 and are today known as Rangers Way. It was down these steps on 5 June 1944 that the 2nd Ranger Battalion, the American army unit under the command of Lt-Col James E. Rudder, descended from their inland camp before falling in on the Promenade and marching to their embarkation point at the harbour near where the Pavilion stands today.

Their final destination was the Pointe du Hoc in Normandy where they were to acquit themselves magnificently in their taking and defending of the headland. Archive pictures of the time show them in good spirits marching along the promenade.

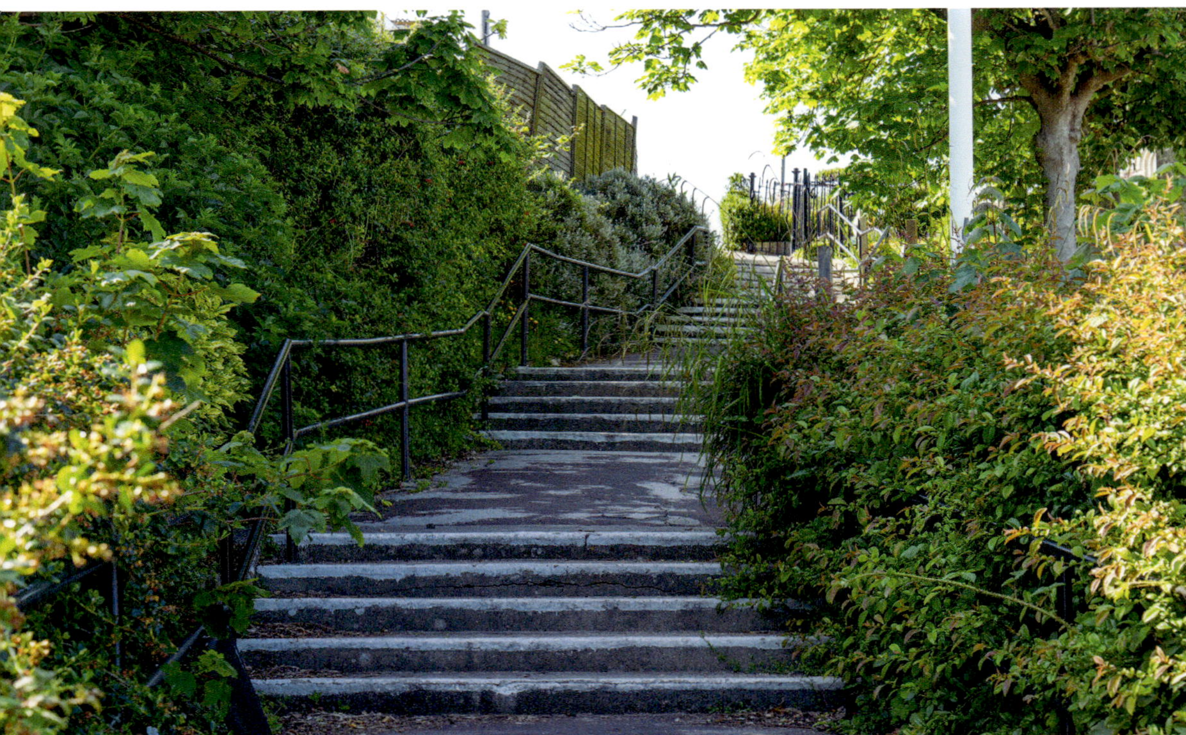

The Rangers Way by Greenhill Gardens.

Railways

Weymouth railway station is in the very centre of town, only a short walk from the seafront (Upwey station, once known as Weymouth junction, which also technically serves Weymouth, stands some miles to the north) and is the terminus station of both the South West Main Line and the Heart of Wessex Line. There are direct links to both Waterloo and Paddington railway stations in London on the South West Main Line and to Bristol Temple Meads and Gloucester on the Heart of Wessex Line.

Such direct connections to large population centres goes some way to explaining the early popularity of Weymouth as a holiday resort and the rapid development in the years before mass personal car ownership.

Plans for the station as part of the Wiltshire, Somerset and Weymouth Railway were first approved in 1845. By the time the station was opened on 20 January 1857 they had been taken over by the Great Western Railway. Lines from Weymouth junction north of town added branch lines to Portland and Weymouth Quay.

The latter would remain in regular use until September 1987, known as the Weymouth Harbour Tramway. It ran on rails in the middle of a busy street where parked cars frequently caused problems for the trains. These trains ran mainly from Waterloo station as part of a boat-trains service. The last train to use the tracks was a Pathfinder Tours charter on 2 May 1999.

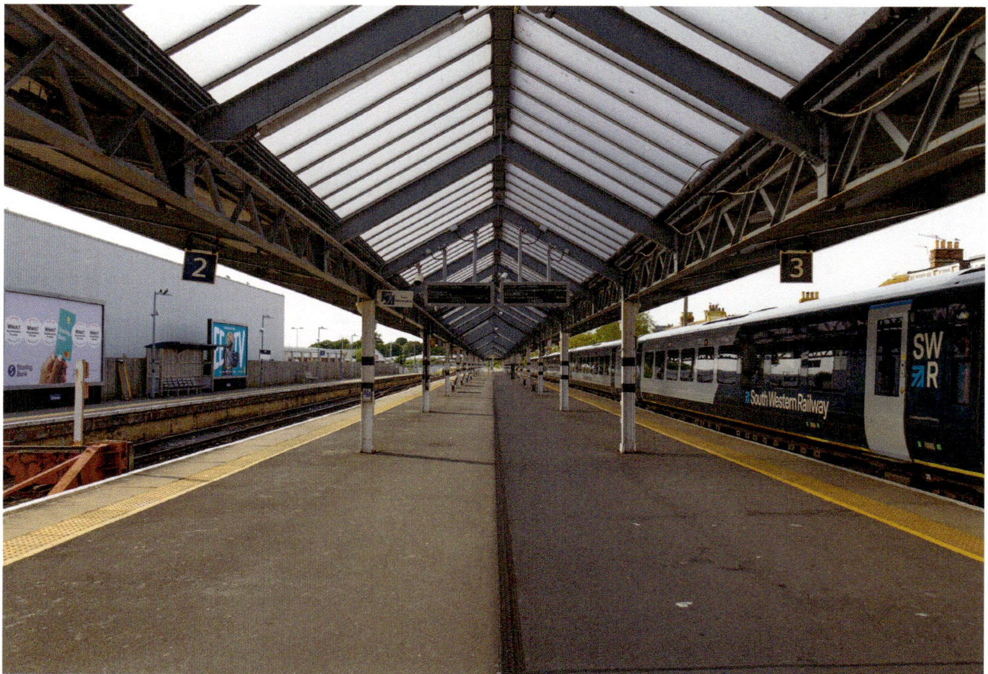

The two long platforms at Weymouth railway station dating from the 1950s.

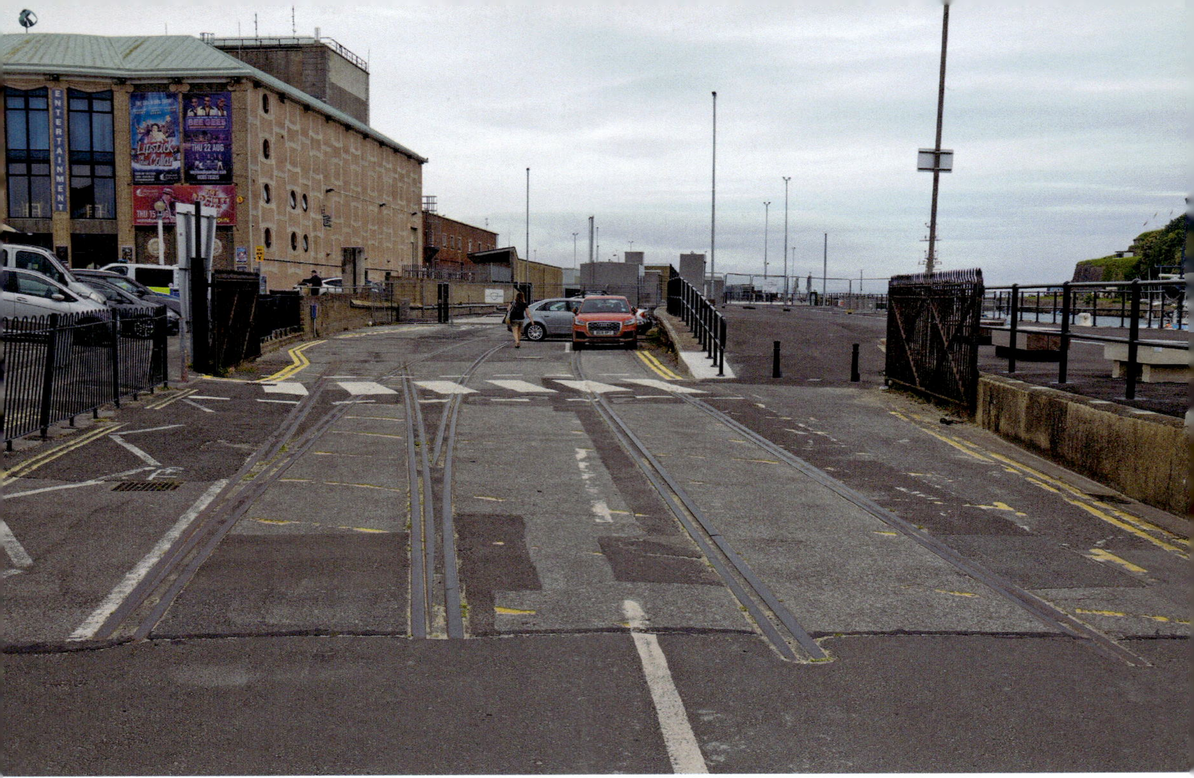

All that remains of the Weymouth harbour tramway, closed in 1999.

Initially classified as 'Out of use: Temporary' by Network Rail, the tracks were finally removed in late 2020 despite calls locally to turn it into part of a tram service. There were briefly thoughts of using the tracks as a way to move people about Weymouth during the Olympics in 2012 but these never came to fruition.

The railway service to Portland would last until 3 March 1952 for passenger traffic with a goods service remaining in place until 9 April 1965. Today the old trackbed is used as a walking trail.

Referred to variously as Weymouth or Weymouth town depending on the timetables publishers at its peak in the early years of the twentieth century, Weymouth station had five platforms with a glazed roof over them, all covering station buildings designed by T. H. Bertram and a large goods yard. There were two engine sheds, one for engines of London and South Western Railway who ran their own line from Dorchester to Weymouth and a larger one for those of the Great Western Railway.

With the large increase in tourist traffic following the Second World War two long-excursion train platforms were installed, and these are the platforms that remain in use today.

The massive increase in excursion traffic was only short-lived and Weymouth station soon found itself too large for the traffic it was required to handle. The goods yard was closed in 1972 and many of the remaining sidings taken up and replaced by a retail park in 1987.

The now far smaller station was rebuilt and reopened on 3 July 1986 at the cost of £750,000 with much-improved modern facilities.

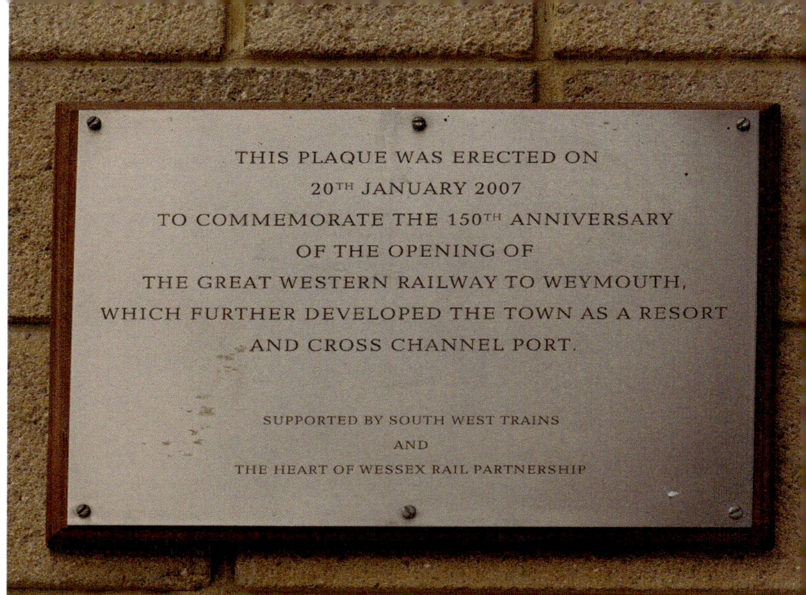

Weymouth station proudly displays this plaque commemorating 150 years of railways in Weymouth.

Royal Hotel

The magnificent architecture of the Royal Hotel on the Esplanade dates back to the Victorian days of the nineteenth century and stands on the site of the original Royal Hotel. This was opened in 1773 as the Stacie hotel and was frequented by King George III whose statue stands nearby, so it was soon renamed in his honour. The original was demolished in 1891 and was replaced by the magnificent building that stands there today.

Designed by Charles Orlando Law, construction began in 1897 and was completed and opened on 16 May 1899. A stone panel is set into the reception desk with the inscription 'The foundation stone of the Royal Hotel Weymouth was laid on the twenty second of April 1987 by Charles Jesty Esq, Mayor. Opened sixteenth May 1899.'

During the Second World War, when Weymouth and the surrounding coastal towns were major embarkation points for the Normandy landings, the Royal Hotel was taken over by the American army in 1943, reopening to the public in 1945.

Predominantly constructed of red Victorian bricks, it has facings of Portland stone which give the building a delightful two-tone look. Made a listed building in 1974, its style is officially described in the listing documents as being in a 'vigorous Northern Renaissance style with Flemish details'.

The entrance door is surrounded by a glorious Portland stone triumphal arch archway and portico. At either side of the building stand octagonal end pavilions (the author was told to stop calling them turrets). Columns styled into the upper floor feature finely rendered lions' heads at their bases.

Unseen at the rear of the building, fronting onto Gloucester Mews, is The Queen's Ballroom and an old coach house – much in demand when the building was constructed, many of the rich arriving in their own carriages.

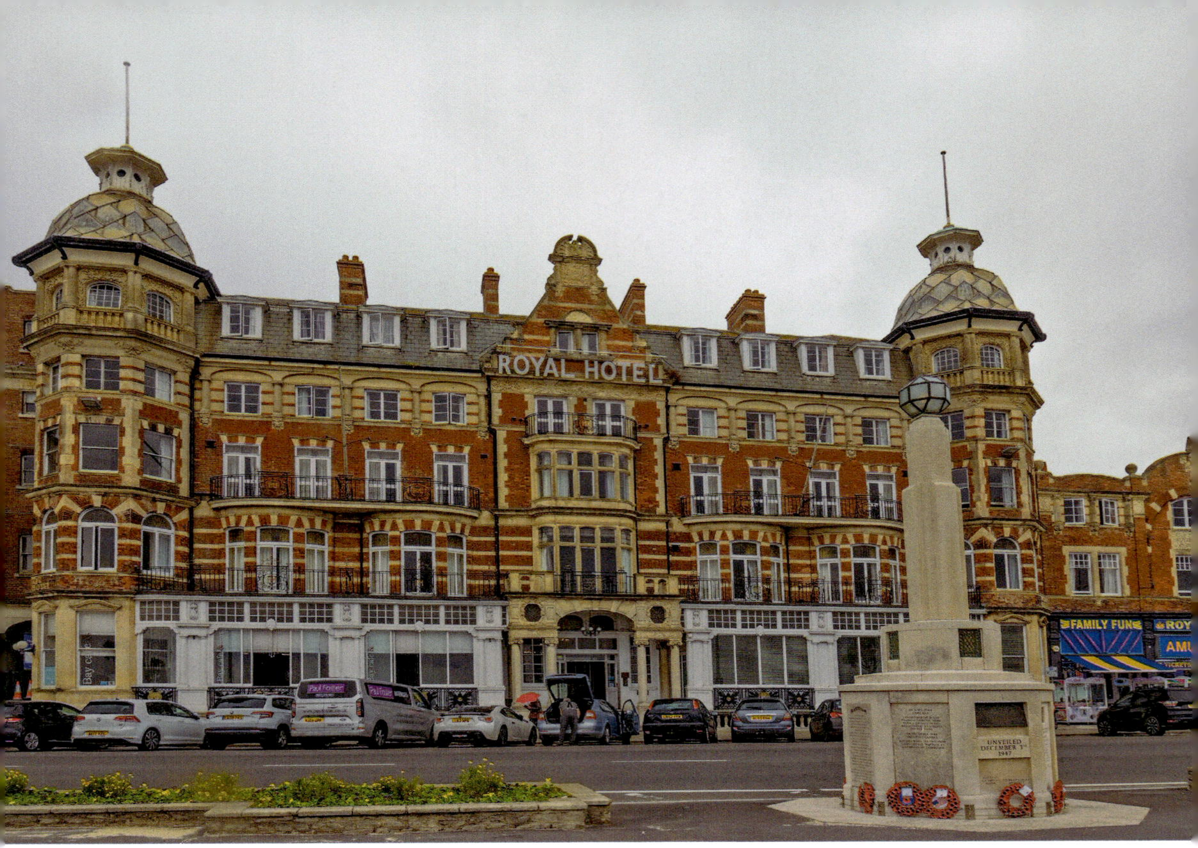

The Royal Hotel with the D-Day memorial in the foreground.

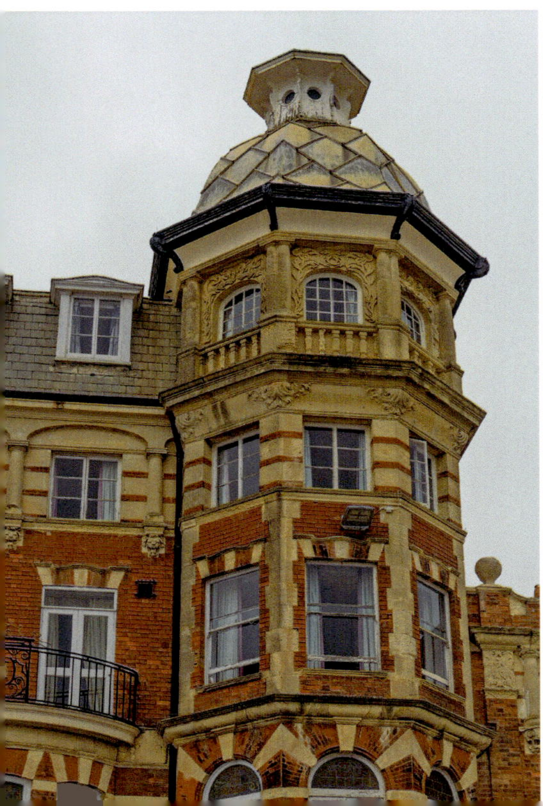

The limestone and granite end pavilion of the
Royal Hotel.

Sandcastles

In common with Weston-super-Mare on the north Somerset coast, Weymouth sand has the properties that make it ideal for the construction of finely detailed sandcastles. For many years (now fast approaching its 100th birthday) there has been an annual display on the Esplanade opposite Alexandra Gardens created by local man Fred Darrington. Looking for all the world like the building was inspired by a science fiction UFO, the display is free to view and attracts hundreds of visitors every year.

The display is created anew every holiday season and usually has some aspect of a seasonal theme. For 2018 there was a strong theme of remembrance as it was the 100th anniversary of the end of the First World War. There have also been displays for the Platinum Jubilee of Queen Elizabeth II and a fantasy display including such luminaries as *Doctor Who*.

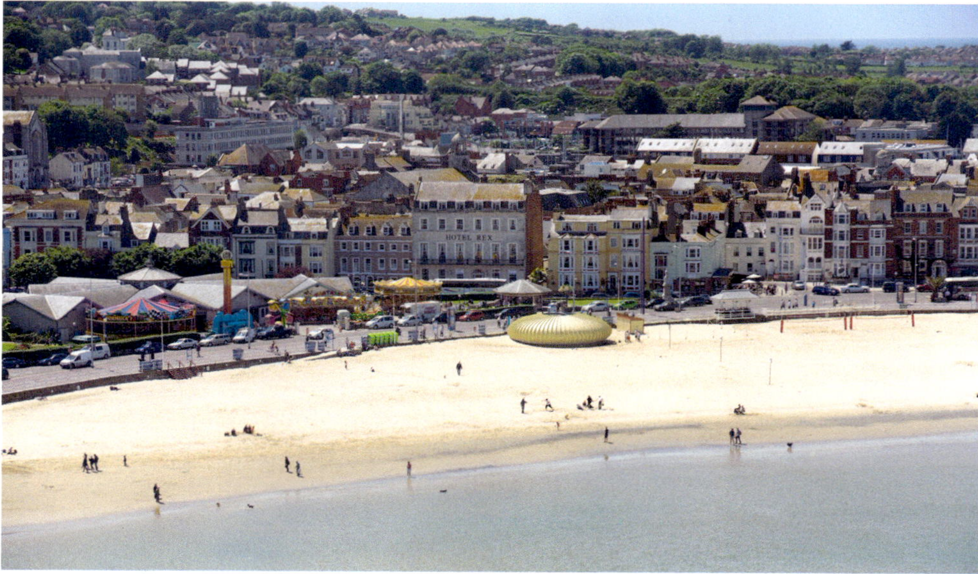

The long-standing seafront sandcastle display building is known locally as 'The UFO'.

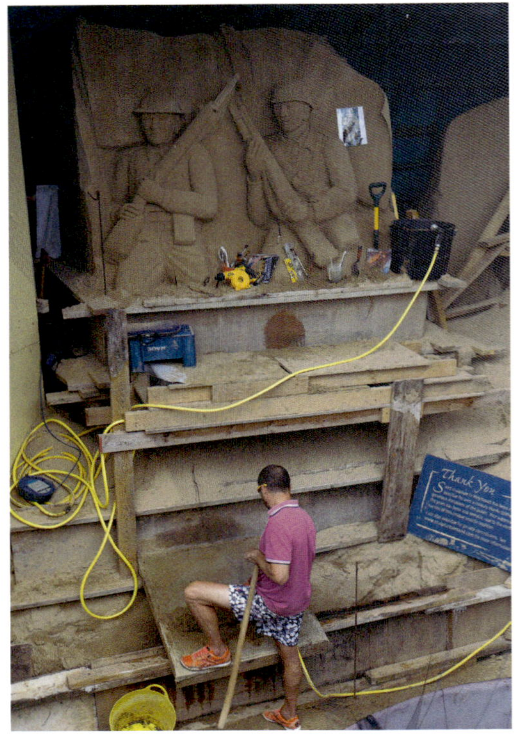

Hand-created from local sand, the exhibits are changed every year.

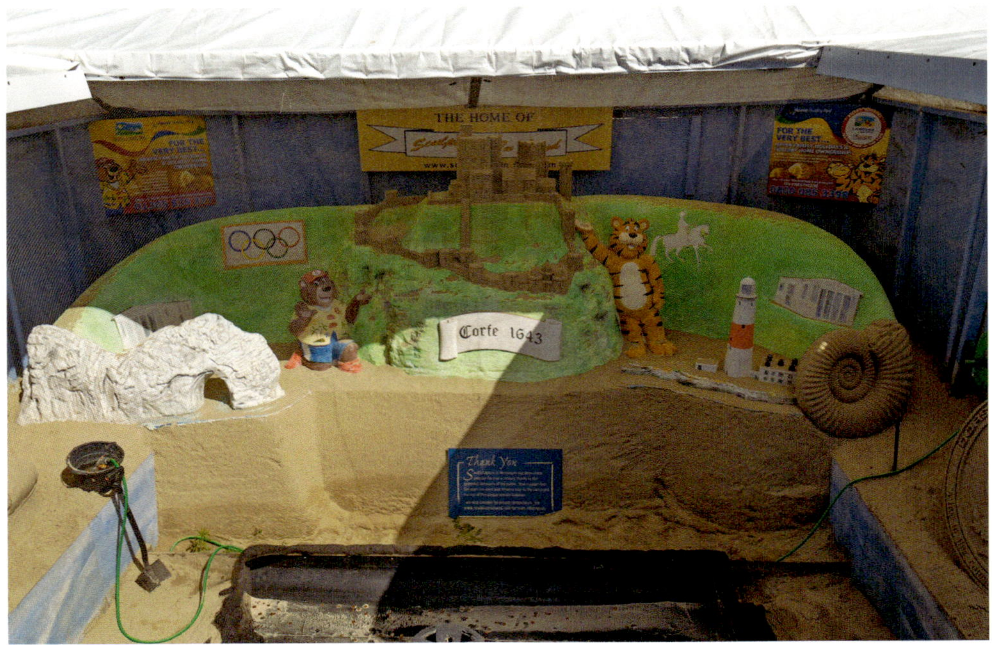

Initially unique to Weymouth was the fact their sandcastles were coloured.

Possibly unique among West Country sand sculptors, Fred Darrington made his displays even more impressive by adding colour to the sand to bring them to life.

Mark Anderson, grandson of the architect of the sandcastles a sand sculptor in his own right having studied under the great man himself, set out to realise a dream to put Weymouth on the world sand sculpture map. With local businessman David Hicks he located a derelict industrial site at the far end of the seafront and in 2011 created 'Sandworld', the UK's only all-weather undercover sandcastle exhibition. The site was swiftly cleared and no fewer than seventy-five lorry loads of sand were imported to the site to create the seasonal sculpture event.

St George's Church

On exiting the road that leads to the Tout Quarry Sculpture Park you might glance to your right and glimpse the striking shape of St George's Church. Once the only parish church on Portland, it has a most unusual shape with an aborted dome and is surrounded by a large and remarkably varied churchyard.

St George's Church was preceded by St Andrew's as the parish church of Portland which began to fall into disrepair during the middle of the sixteenth century. A survey in August 1753 found that the cost of refurbishing St Andrew's would be over half the cost of building a new church, and as its location was both not ideal for many of the parishioners and built on unstable land, a plan was made to build a new church.

A design was chosen by local architect and quarry owner Thomas Gilbert, and construction using locally quarried Portland stone began in 1754. Completed and consecrated in 1766, it replaced St Andrew's Church and remained in use until 1914 when it was allowed to fall into disrepair until the 1960s.

A local group, Friends of St George's Church, raised funds for a restoration during the 1960s, and when the church was declared to be redundant in April 1970 it was placed in the care of the Churches Conservation Trust in 1971.

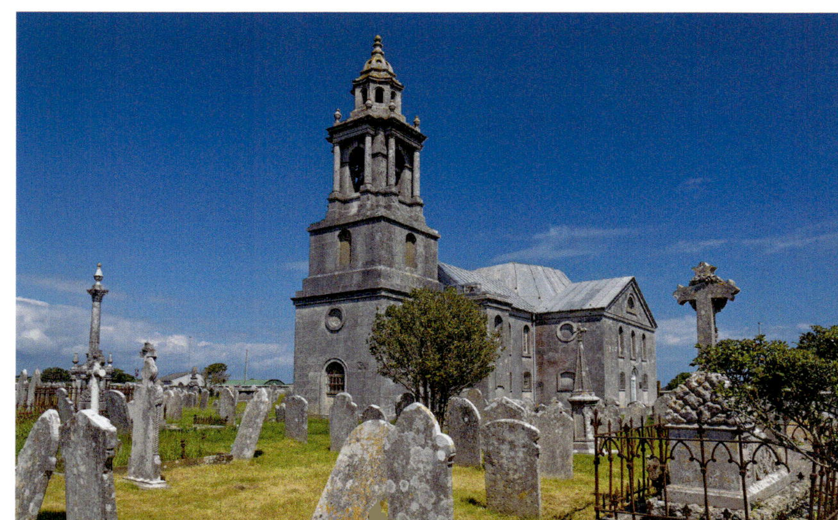

St George's Church on Portland.

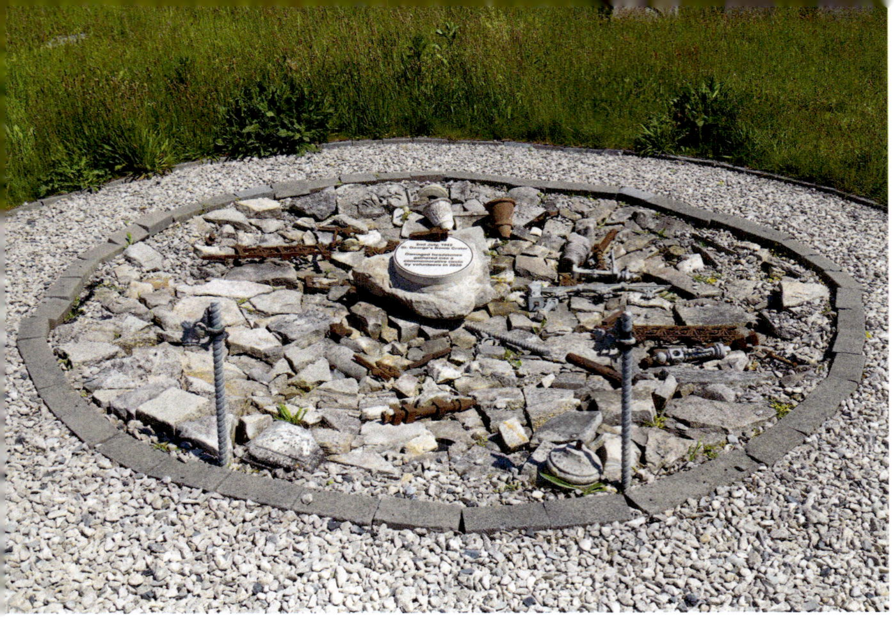

The preserved site of a German bomb crater at St George's Church on Portland.

The restored interior of the church remains well preserved with two levels of pews and an unusual twin pulpit design. One was designated for the reading of the scriptures and the other for the preaching of lengthy sermons.

The vast and densely packed churchyard outside includes graves and memorials for such notables as Richard Otter who was lost on the *Titanic* and the Reverend William Robert Morris Waugh, the famous astronomer. The rumour that one notable gravestone prominently displaying the scull and cross bones is that of a local pirate is sadly a myth, but the headstone remains remarkable to behold.

During the Second World War on 2 July 1942 a bomb no doubt intended for the prominent harbour below landed in the churchyard of St George's Church causing considerable damage. The church no longer being in active use, the damage and crater was left untended until 2020 when volunteers gathered together all the damaged headstones into a commemorative circle on the site of the crater. This memorial circle remains lovingly cleared and cared for.

Today, officially classified as redundant, the church only holds two services per year, one on St George's Day and one on Christmas Day.

The church was given listed status in January 1951.

St Mary's Church

As you walk down the pedestrian-friendly portals of St Mary Street and look south towards the harbour you will see on the left, towering above the other buildings and likely hiding behind the trees, the bell and clock tower of St Mary's Church. With an unusual frontal design of three doors beneath three arched windows, the tower is visible from miles around as it stands above all the surrounding buildings.

Today it is grand building faced with the traditional local Portland stone (described by Historic England as being in 'an austere design of Palladian node' around a brick core),

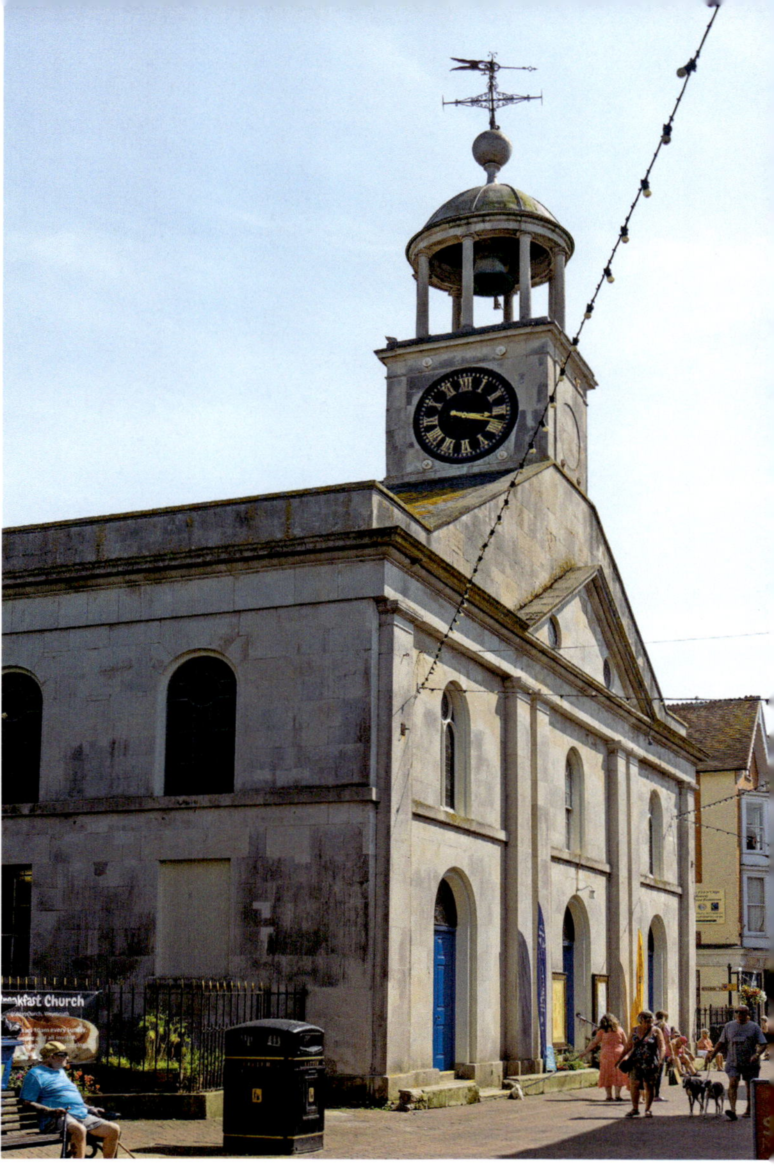

St Mary's Church standing
on St Mary Street,
Weymouth.

but it was not always thus. The first chapel on the site was recorded as far back as 1299 as a small chantry chapel where fishermen could pray before departing to sea.

A new church was built on the site in 1605 along with adjoining land to form the churchyard we see today. In 1606 this replaced St Mary's Church in Radipole as the local parish church. This decision was made as the church in Radipole was considered too small for the existing and fast-growing congregation and in a location many found difficult to access.

The new church was frequented by King George III during his visits to Weymouth, and he continued to rent a Royal Pew for many years, both in this and the later incarnation of the church.

When the congregation outgrew the old church the old building was demolished in 1815 and a foundation stone laid for the church you see today by the Bishop of

Salisbury, the Right Reverend John Fisher, on 4 October. It was designed to hold 2,000 worshipers, with many seats set aside specifically for the poor of the parish and visitors to the town. James Hamilton, a local architect, drew up the plans and an Act of Parliament set construction in motion in June 1815.

The new church was opened by the Reverend Doctor England, Archdeacon of Dorset on 23 March 1817. A further rebuilding and renovation in 1922 saw the fitting of electric lights to the church and a rebuilding of the Northern Aisle.

Inside the church the space is dominated by a painting of the Last Supper on the reredos (a screen behind the altar) by local-born artist Sir James Thornhill. This was presented to the church in 1721 when the artist became an MP for the town.

More famous for his large-scale paintings in places like the inside of the dome of St Paul's Cathedral in London and a ceiling at Blenheim Palace, finding a piece of his work in such a small parish church comes as a surprise to many.

Originally known as Christ Church, the church only became known as St Mary's when the new building was opened in 1817. There was already a church dedicated to St Mary locally at Radipole, and eventually this became known as St Ann's, but some records show it as still being known as St Mary's as late as 1926 when Radipole and Melcombe Regis (as this area of modern-day Weymouth was known) became separate parishes and the current St Mary's became the official parish church.

St Mary's Church became a listed building in December 1953.

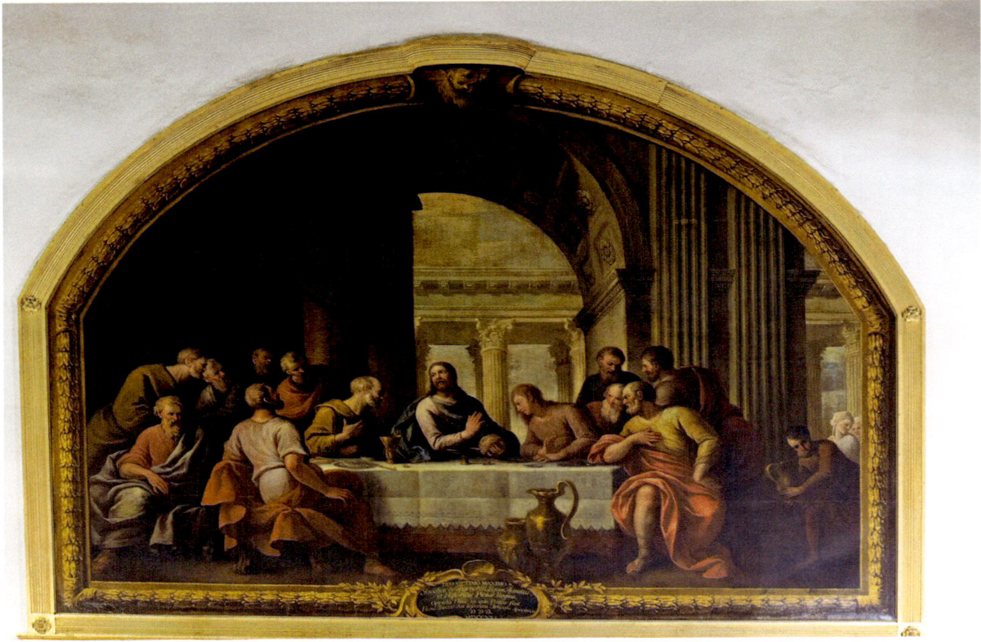

'The Last Supper' by Sir James Thornhill at St Mary's Church.

T

Tout Quarry Sculpture Park

High atop the Isle of Portland and accessed through a trading estate lies Tout Quarry. It is positioned on top of the western cliffs of Portland, the name referring to the location, roughly translating from Latin as 'Look out'.

Tout Quarry was worked commercially since the middle of the eighteenth century and was one of several quarries working along the West Cliffs (others included Trade, Bowers and Inmosthay quarries), moving slowly inwards as the demand for Portland stone increased. The quarry was served by its own cable and horse-drawn railway and tramway system from 1862, by which time the fashionable Portland stone was being shipped all over the world.

Lano's Arch, built in 1854 by Jonathan Comben Lano in the very centre of the quarry to carry the railway over a ravine, was part of this system and still stands today and is now a listed feature. Lano would sadly meet his end during a riot between locals and a Royal Navy press-gang; he was killed by a musket ball.

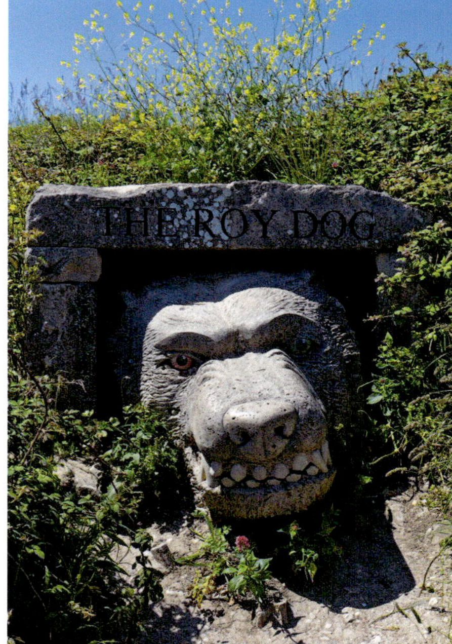

'The Roy Dog' famous sculpture at Tout Quarry Sculpture Park on Portland.

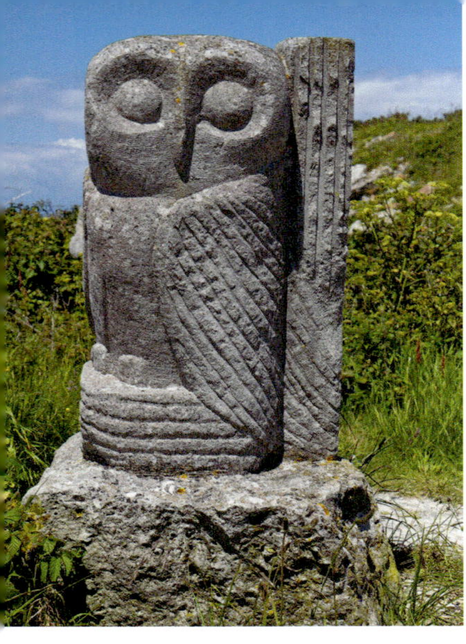

The Owl sculpture at the park.

Traditionally, Tout Quarry was spilt along several operators, each producing different types of Portland stone. As some of these types required over 30 feet of 'waste' stone to be removed before the desired layer was reached, the tramway within the quarry took vast amounts of 'waste' stone to the edge of Portland and dumped it to form the still clearly visible scree slopes at West Weare below.

During the Second World War the quarry was taken over as part of the Chain Home Low radar chain and a radar station constructed. The radar station tracked both planes and shipping, being initially manned by the army, then taken over by the Royal Air Force and finally by the Royal Navy as part of the Cold War ROTOR system for early warning defence. Now only the old drill hall remains of the radar station, and is used for annual courses in stone sculpture.

The commercial extraction of stone ended in 1982 when 30,000 tons of stone were quarried for a single contract for coastal defence purposes, and in 1983 the Portland Quarry and Sculpture Trust was formed with the avowed intention of 'preserving a knowledge and understanding of all aspects of stone and the landscape from which it comes' and 're-establishing the spirit of creativity in the Portland quarries'.

They created what was the UK's first sculpture quarry. They were leased the quarry by the owners, Kingston Minerals, and the guiding inspiration for the new sculpture park was local resident Jonathan Phipps. They invited sculptors from all over the world to create sculptures to the now empty quarry. At the time of writing there are around seventy, ranging from flat structures carved directly into the rock faces to numerous three-dimensional and free-standing sculptures. Keen and energetic visitors can download a map and tour them all. If you manage to find them all on your first visit, you are doing better than the author.

In 2012 the quarry was also designated a nature reserve managed by the Dorset Wildlife Trust who also look after the adjoining King Barrow Quarry nature reserve. Many low, slow-growing plants, lichens and small wildlife have flourished in the now quiet limestone environment, most notably the unique to Portland silver-studded blue butterfly and the bee orchid.

The quarry came runner-up in the 2008 British Urban Regeneration Association awards for community-inspired regenerations and was shortlisted for the British Urban Regeneration awards scheme in 2009.

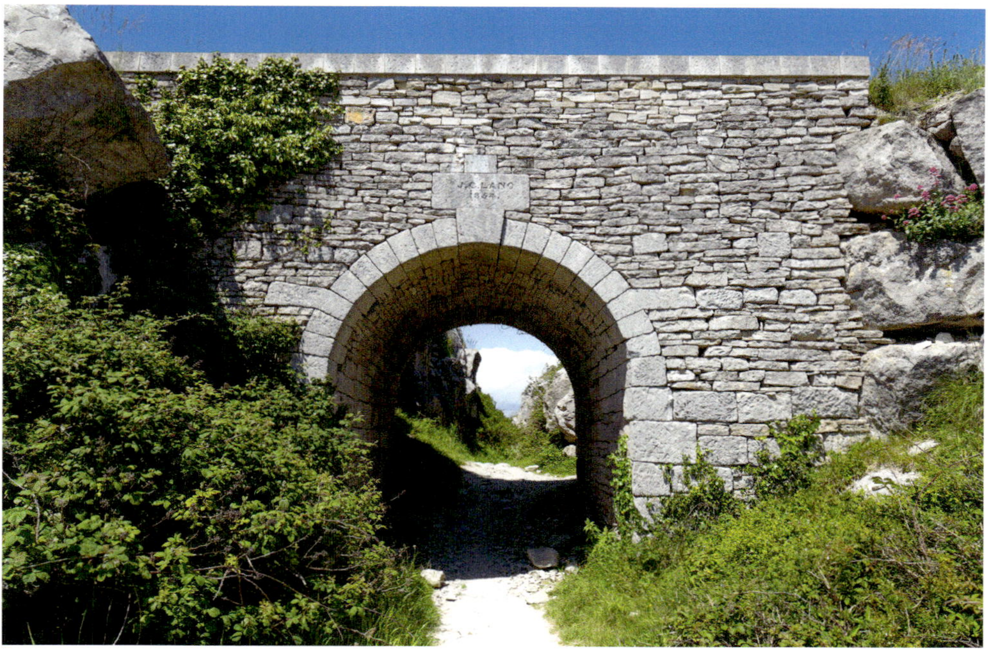

Lano's Arch, dating from 1854, at the park.

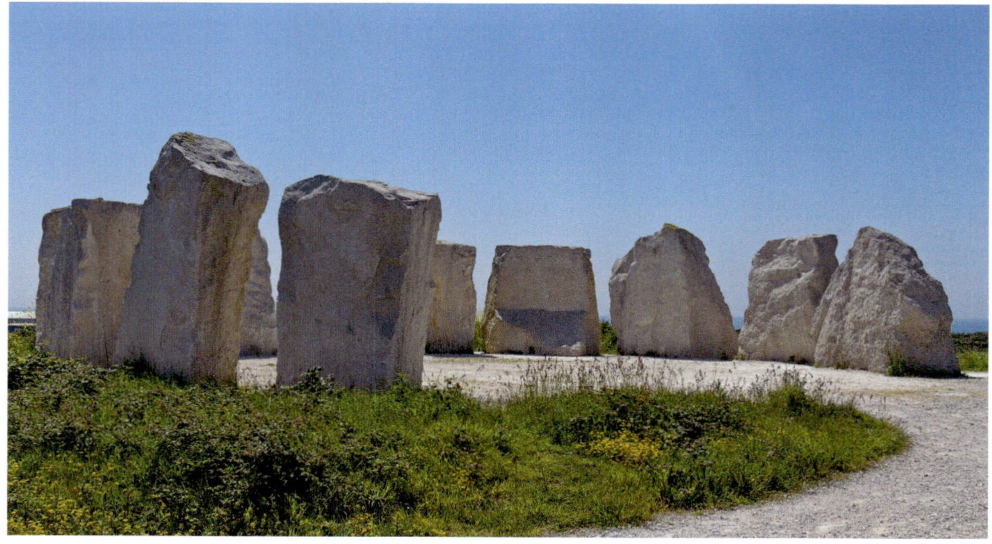

A stone circle created from waste blocks on Portland.

Town Bridge

The magnificent Town Bridge links the sides of the harbour that were once separate –Melcombe Regis and Weymouth. To allow the river and harbour traffic to flow freely the bridge opens the two sections roughly every two hours every day of the year and at extra times during the holiday season to allow the ever-increasing flow of leisure traffic to go about their businesses. Every raising of the bridge is guaranteed to pull a crowd of local and tourists to watch the silent lifting of the roadway and to await what boat will appear beneath.

The Town Bridge takes its design inspiration from Tower Bridge in London in that it is a twin-leaf (two sections of roadway or arms that can be raised) bascule bridge. Each leaf of the bascule weighs approximately 200 tons but is carefully designed and balanced to allow them to be raised by a relatively small electric motor powering the hydraulic system.

The foundation stone for the current bridge was laid in April 1929 by the town mayor, Percy Boyle. The general construction work was carried out by Bolton and Larkin Ltd with the steelwork supply contract being awarded to the Cleveland Bridge and Engineering Company of Darlington whose steelwork can be seen in memorable bridges all over the world. Given its central and very obvious location in the very middle of the town, the bridge was carefully designed to look dignified when approached from either side and is painted in the colours of Weymouth in common with many other landmarks in the town.

The roadway is lit by six magnificent iron lights set atop the various stone pillars in what is referred to as an open pyramid style with a trellis top by Historic England. They appear in what the author considers a nautical style and certainly add something

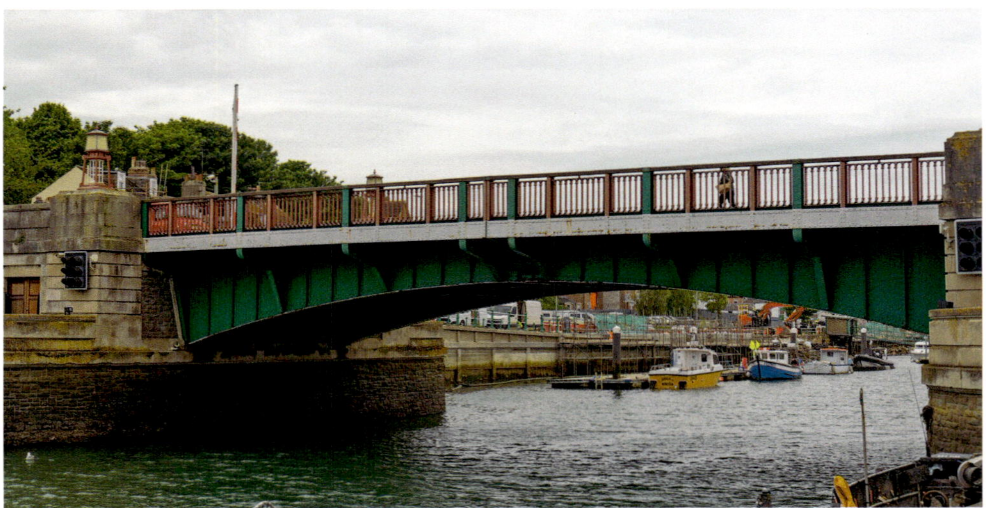

Weymouth Town Bridge.

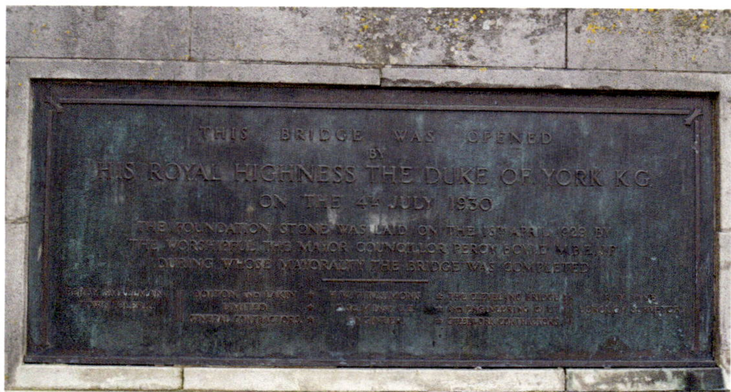

The bronze plaque dedicating the opening of Weymouth Town Bridge.

to the look of the bridge, painted – as is the rest of the iron work – in traditional Weymouth colours.

The octagonal control room with a window on each face is clearly visible at one end of the roadway and much of the stationary parts of the bridge are clad in the traditional-for-the-area Portland stone mixed with grey-sandstone blocks.

Sheltered walkways from the lower level of the harbour up to the level of the road were built into the plan for pedestrians from the very start and still see heavy foot traffic today.

The bridge was completed in 1930 at a cost of £90,000, or roughly three million pounds in today's terms. This vast investment was split between the Borough Council, the County Council and the government's Ministry of Transport.

The roadway was first raised on 4 July 1930 by HRH The Duke of York (later King George VI) when he personally operated the electric switches to raise the roadway and allow the Cosen's paddle steamer *Empress* carrying a special party of schoolchildren to pass beneath. This event, and all the people and companies who were involved with the contraction of the bridge, are commemorated on a large bronze plaque on its seaward side.

On the opposite side, set into the stonework is an unusual block of granite inscribed 'From Weymouth New England to Weymouth Old England: 1930', a gift from Weymouth harbour in Nova Scotia when the bridge was under construction.

The current Town Bridge is the last in the long line of bridges at this vital location between the two sets of buildings either side of the active harbour location stretching back to 1597 when the first bridge replaced the old rope ferry.

All the early bridges were of wood, suffering damage during the English Civil War (of which more elsewhere under the 'Cannonball' entry) and being rebuilt no fewer than three times –in 1713, 1741 and 1770. A stone bridge was finally built in 1824 and at one point a toll was charged for its use, there being a toll house on the Melcombe Regis side.

This stone structure was updated during the 1890s but by the 1920s it was deemed unsuitable for the level of traffic the busy harbour and rising number of residents was now creating. The result of the following consultation is the bridge that still stands here today.

In 2023 the bridge was closed for nearly three months while the steel roadway was effectively removed, all the welds checked and replaced as required. Considering the bridge roadway had been untouched since the 1930 opening, this must be considered a testament to the original building works.

Like many of the striking structures of Weymouth, the Town Bridge was given listed status in 1997.

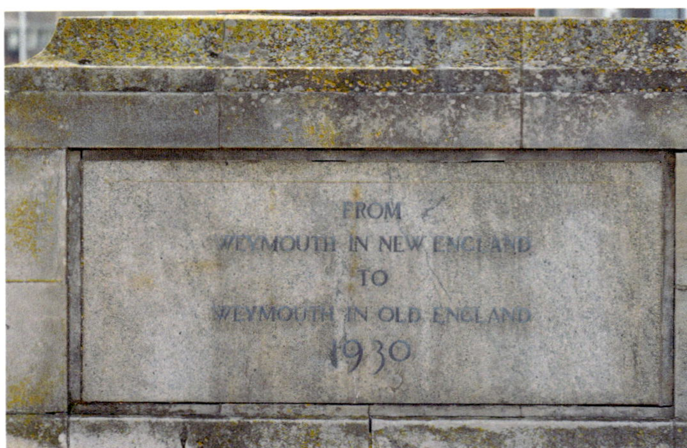

A granite block on Weymouth bridge from their namesake town in New England.

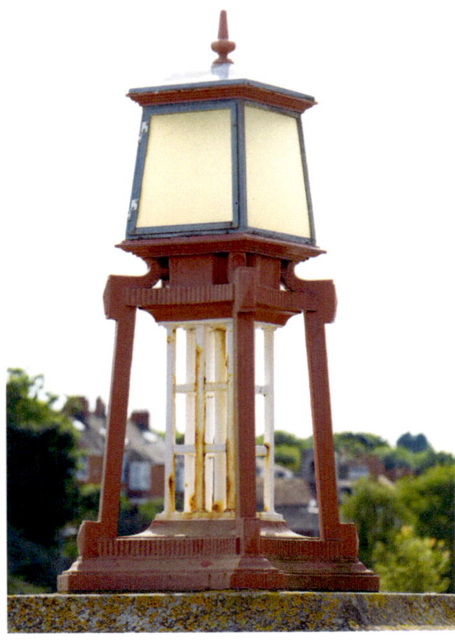

Nautical art deco-style lamps on Weymouth Town Bridge.

Underpass Murals

In an attempt to brighten up the depressing Westham underpass in October 2007 and to deter other graffiti scrawlers, Weymouth and Portland Borough Council commissioned local youngsters with £7,000 to produce brightly coloured murals inspired by childhood and the local area.

There are murals depicting contemporary dance, Airfix toy soldiers, some seaside rock and a very large seagull sufficient to put the fear of God into any holidaymaker.

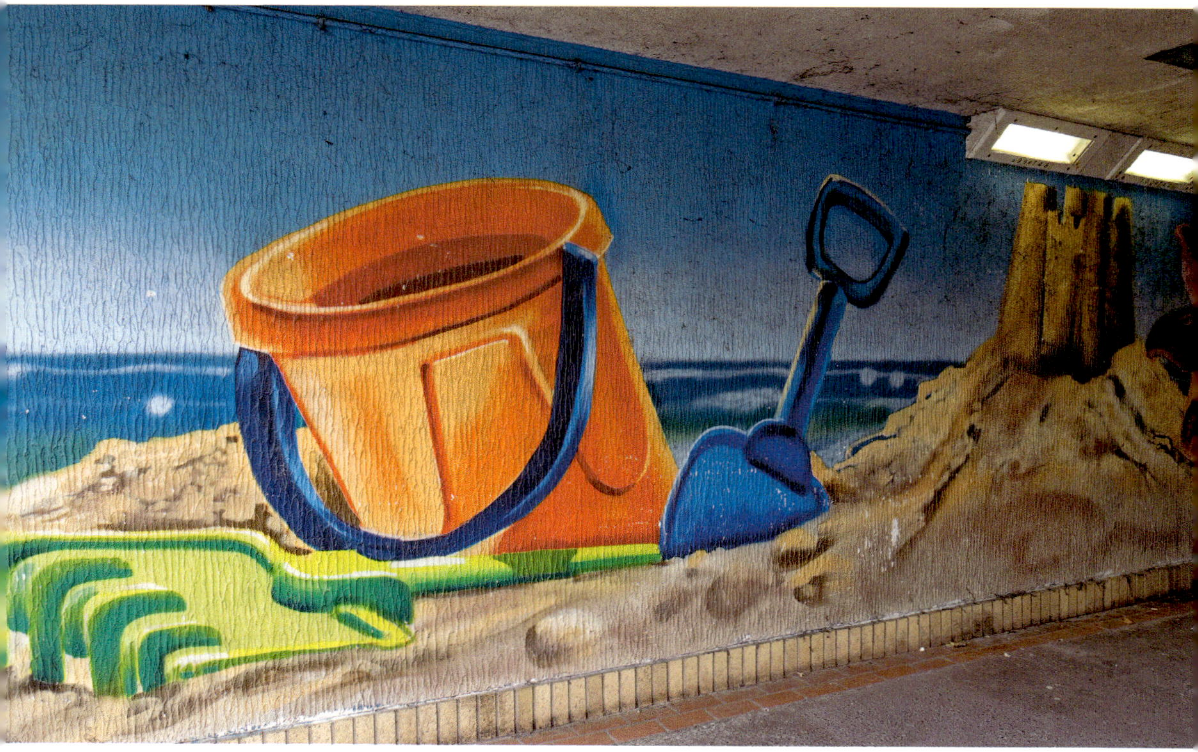

Brightly coloured underpass murals of seaside scenes.

Verne Citadel

Approached through a magnificent Victorian gateway of local Portland stone (you will likely have time to examine it as traffic through it is controlled by traffic lights as the road is too narrow for two vehicles to pass), at the end of a number of savage switchback turns, Verne Citadel was designed as a 'siege fort' standing on the very top of Portland on Verne Hill, after which the Citadel is named. It stands on the site of an Iron Age hill fort, and the Roman's occupied the site later. In 1798, as the English watched the upheaval in Revolutionary France, a naval signal station was placed on top of Portland as part of a chain to monitor shipping in the Channel.

It was constructed between 1858 and 1881 to a design by Captain W. Crossman of the Royal Engineers. When completed the Citadel enclosed and area of around 56 acres. Portland Prison was established to provide convict labour for the Admiralty quarries required for these construction projects and Verne Citadel was constructed using a mixture of convict labour and local contractors, all under the command of Royal Engineers.

Its original purpose was to provide protection for shipping and naval ships in the new Royal Navy harbour being created below with two new breakwaters and on the Portland Roads approaches. It was to be the harbour's main defensive fortification, with the field of fire of the guns covering their approaches.

As a fortification in its own right the Citadel was unapproachable from the north and east, and protection from assault to the south and west sides was provided by the digging of deep ditches. Nearly 70 feet deep and one 120 feet wide in places, the excavated stone (nearly 1.5 million tons of it) was used in the construction of the breakwaters around the new harbour. Extra protection was provided to the Citadel by the East Weare battery and camp, considered by the military to be parts of the main fortification.

Designed with open gun platforms on north, east and southern sides, the Citadel was, at its height, armed with 12.5-inch breech-loading guns supported by a whole array of lighter guns. Never actually firing a shot in anger, the Citadel was decommissioned as part of the UK's coastal defence fortifications in 1906 but continued in military ownership for many years.

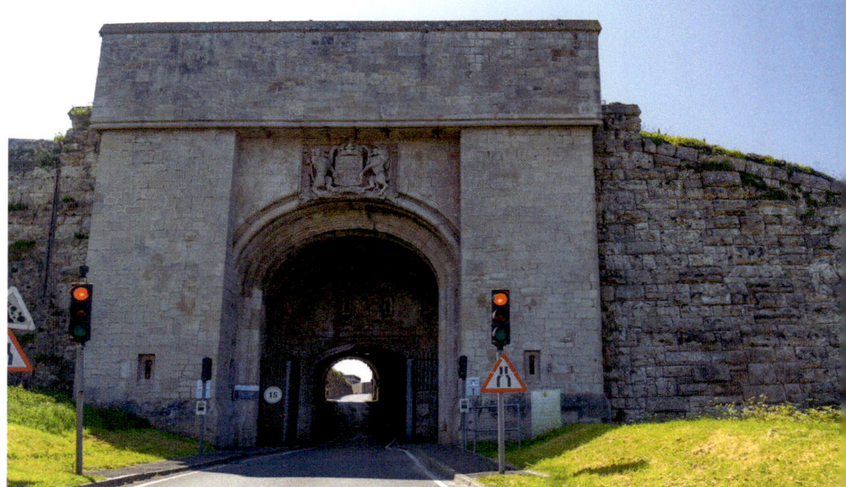

The mighty fortified entrance to Verne Citadel.

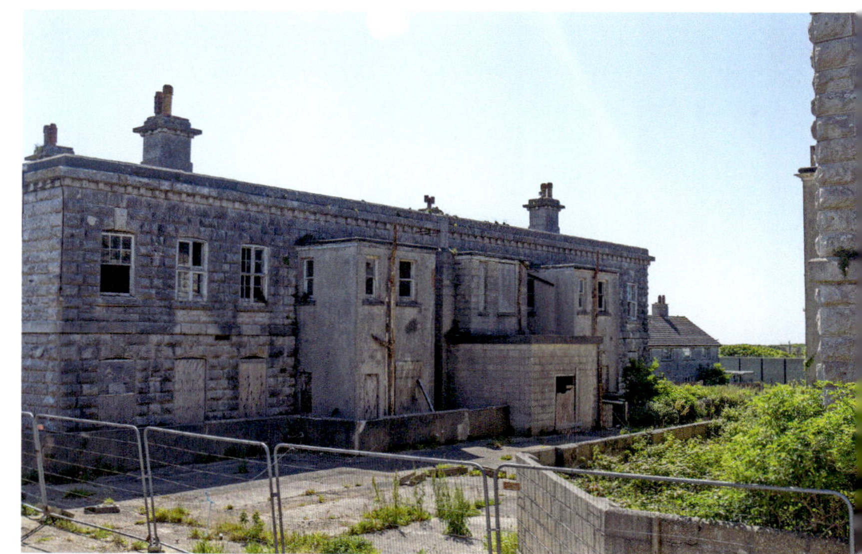

Disused period buildings inside what is now HMP Verne.

During the First Wold War it would serve as a heavy anti-aircraft battery armed with a Hotchkiss gun, a munitions store and from 1917 a hospital for wounded ANZAC soldiers returning from Gallipoli. The former role would be repeated during the Second World War when the Citadel would again be occupied by a battery of 3.7-inch heavy anti-aircraft guns and a radar station. Such was the height of Portland that the radar station could be used to track both airborne and seaborne targets.

After the Second World War the Citadel would become the home of HMP The Verne from February 1949 until January 2014, briefly being used as an immigration detention centre from 2014–17, then returning to use as a prison in 2018. At the time of writing as part of the rehabilitation programme prisoners run the excellent 'Jailhouse tea rooms' which offers wonderful views out over the harbour towards Weymouth.

Various parts of Verne Citadel have been listed and protected by Historic England from 1978 onwards and sadly have on occasions been described as being 'at risk'

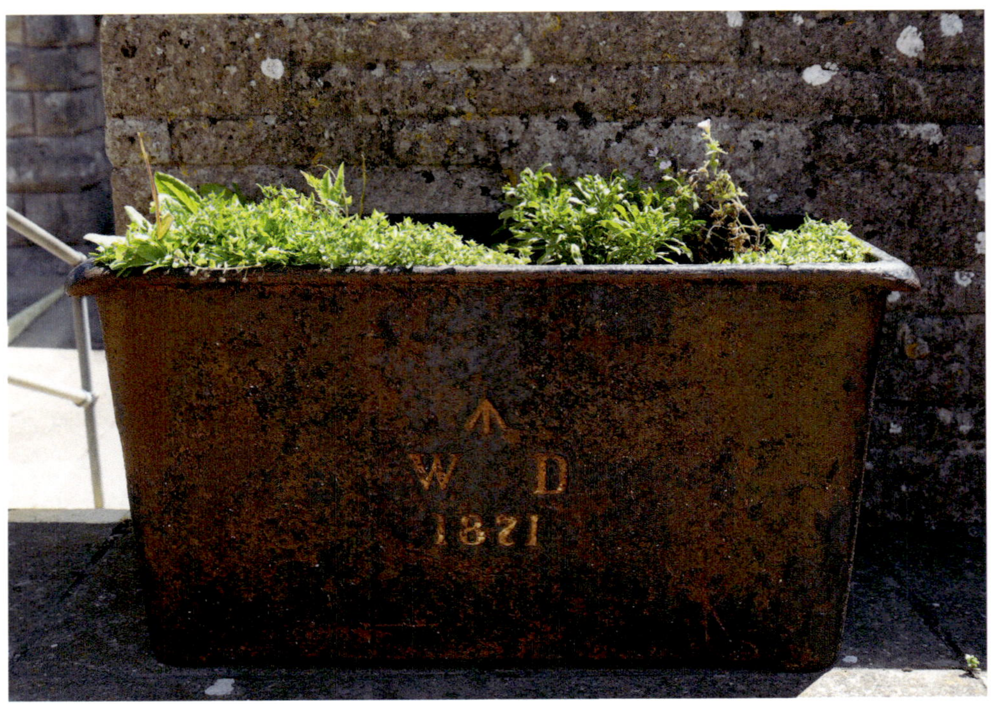

A repurposed iron storage bin displays the original War Department 1821 markings.

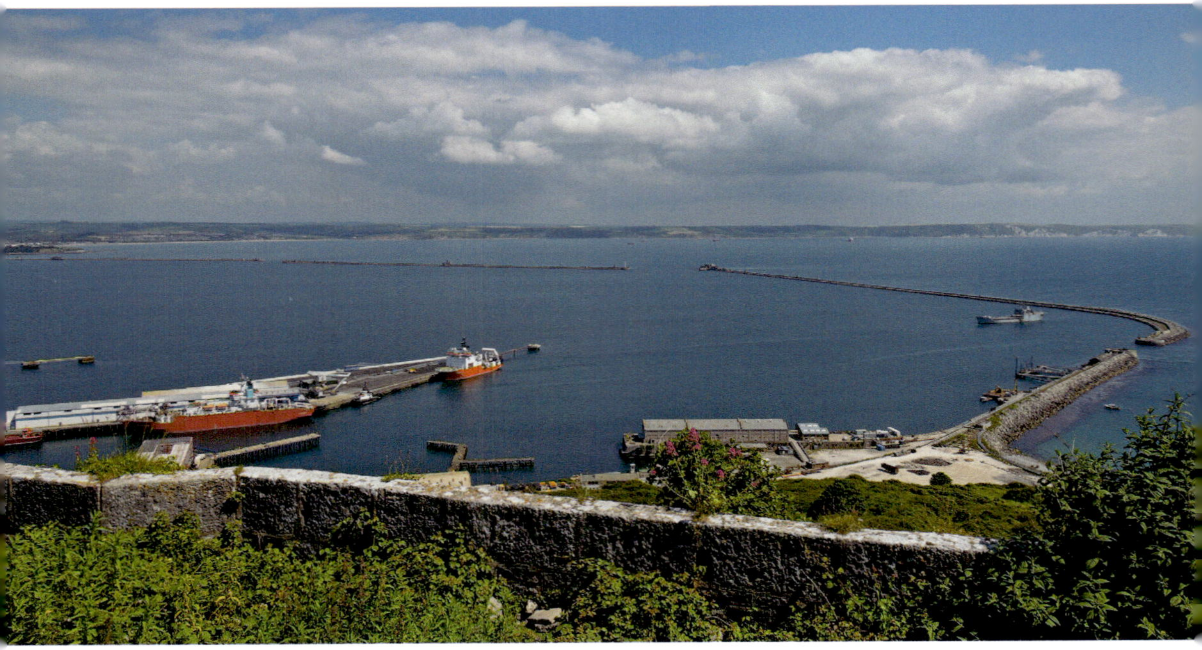

The view of the breakwater and harbour from Jailhouse tearoom at HMP Verne.

Victorian Shelters

Along the Esplanade you will find seven relics of Weymouth from the days of Queen Victoria in the form of surprisingly large pedestrian shelters. Initially these stood at the edge of the Esplanade near to the beach with their own railed balconies, but subsequent expansions of the pavement has seen them effectively moved back from the beach.

Installed in around 1889 from cast-iron parts supplied by Jeffreys of Westminster (a plaque still remaining affixed to one of the shelters gives an address for them of 10 Great Queen Street, Westminster), they were to provide shelter to visitors in the early days of Weymouth as a resort.

They feature a lead over wood-beam roof, interior glazing to protect people from the prevailing winds and period blue-painted wooden seats. The edges of the roofs are decorated with a remarkable fringe of frilly iron work and the roof interior is supported by diagonal iron 'Dragon beams'. All were granted Grade II listed status in December 1997 and as recently as 2018 Weymouth council has had the shelters refurbished to ensure they looked smart and ready for continued use well into the twenty-first century.

Despite their age and some people complaining of their 'dated' look, they remain popular and getting a seat during the tourist season remains a challenge for visitors and locals alike.

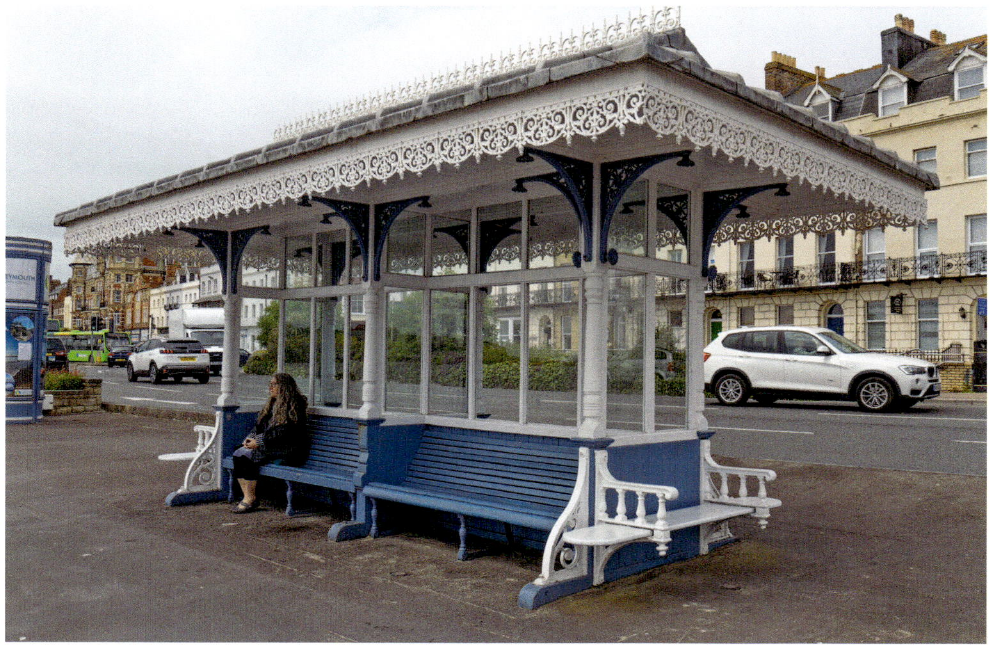

One of seven surprisingly spacious Victorian shelters on Weymouth Esplanade.

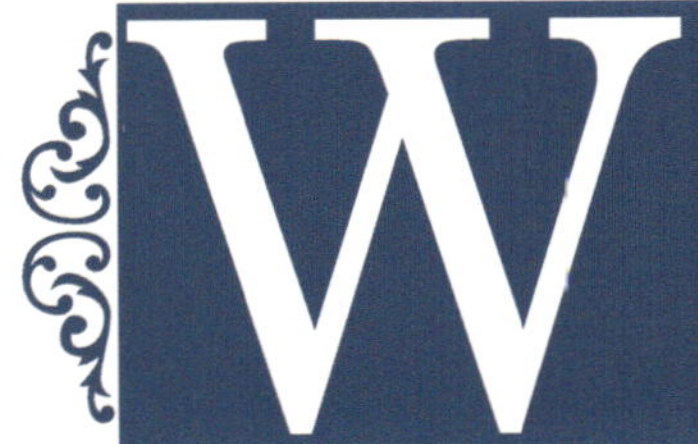

War Memorial

Weymouth has no fewer than four memorials to the fallen of the two World Wars on the Esplanade. Here we are discussing the 'official' memorial opposite the Hotel Prince Regent and near the junction of the Esplanade and Brunswick Terrace and the adjoining memorial bed.

It is a tall, slender column of Portland stone with a sculpture of a traditional laurel wreath on the front face (land-facing side) and a depiction of Christ being supported by angels on the rear face. Within the wreath are the dates 1914–19, the dates of the First World War, which all assumed would never be allowed to happen again. Sadly, they were wrong.

Bronze plaques listing the 387 fallen of the First World War make up the upper section, and smaller bronze plaques are mounted below them listing the 351 fallen of the Second World War.

It was unveiled on 6 November 1921, with the plaques to the fallen of the Second World War unveiled on 8 May 1949. Once free-standing and approachable by the public, the monument now has a low iron fence about it to protect it and to keep in place the wreaths laid regularly at the base.

The war memorial stands alongside a low flower bed-style memorial to other wars and actions in which Weymouth people were involved but that do not have singular memorials. Proud plaques in the front of this memorial bed remember the action at Dieppe, the Korean War of 1950–53 and the Aden conflict.

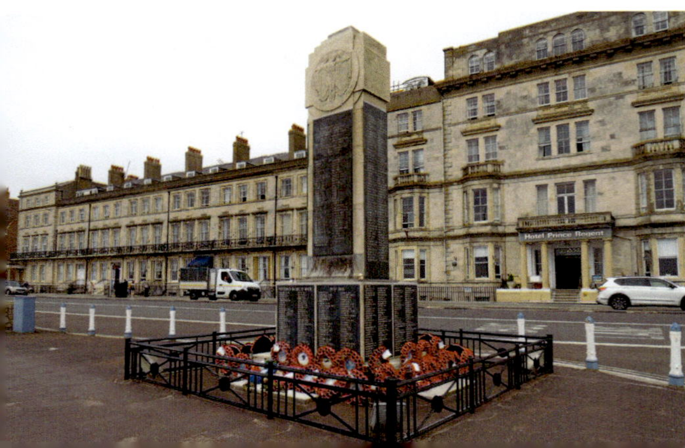

The traditional war memorial on the Esplanade.

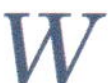

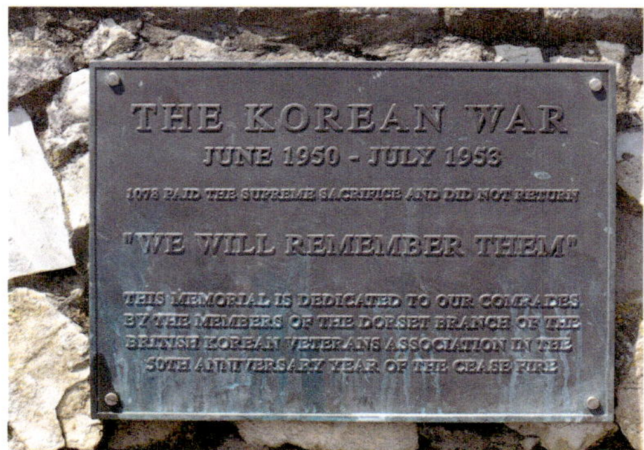

A memorial plaque dedicated to the fallen of the Korean War.

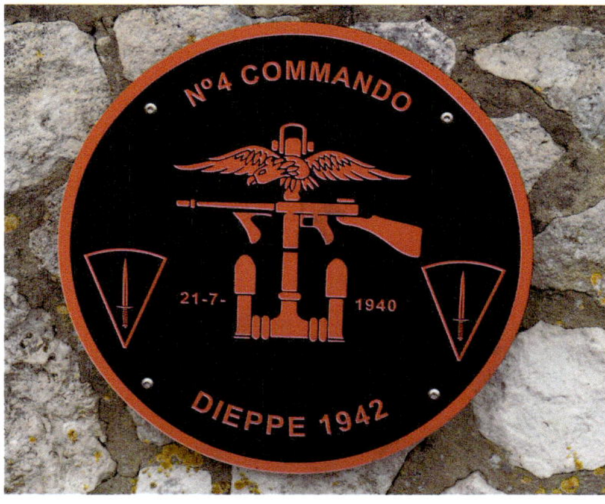

The action at Dieppe is remembered with a plaque on the adjoining memorial flower bed.

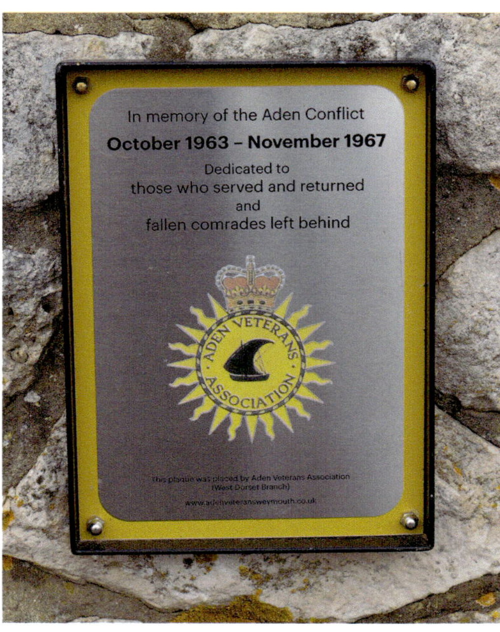

A plaque to mark the largely forgotten Aden conflict on the memorial flower bed.

Weathervane

While wandering the delights of Greenhill Gardens you might be excused for not looking up from the brilliantly coloured flower planting and seeing an unusual memorial.

On top of a stone column atop a tablet of Portland stone is a weathervane in the shape of a 1930s seaplane. Accurately coloured for the period, this is a memorial to Flight Lieutenant (Later Wing Commander) George Hedley Stainforth's world record air speed flight of 406.92 miles per hour reached in a Schneider Supermarine S6B seaplane on 28 September 1931. As a member of the Royal Air Force's high-speed flight he would hold this record more than once in different aircraft, but his final achievements with the modified Supermarine S6B remains his best-remembered hour when he became the first man to travel at over 400 miles per hour, a feat for which he was awarded the Air Force Cross in October 1931.

Sadly, Stainforth did not return from the Second World War, dying in a night-time sortie over the Western Desert in 1941 flying a Bristol Beaufighter. He is buried at the British Cemetery at Ismailia in Egypt.

The weathervane was originally presented to Weymouth College in 1932, a year after the famous world air speed record flight as Stainforth had been a student at the college from 1915–17. Constructed of a copper protective covering over a hardwood frame, the weathervane flew from the college chapel until being removed during the Second World War. After the war the memorial was presented to the council and erected in the gardens in 1952.

The memorial was allowed to fall into disrepair through the rough effects of the sea air and regular battering from salt water and was restored through the intervention of the council in 2014 to the wonderful condition you see today.

His name also lives on within the RAF as every year his family presents the Stainforth Trophy to the strike command squadron that has produced the highest performance.

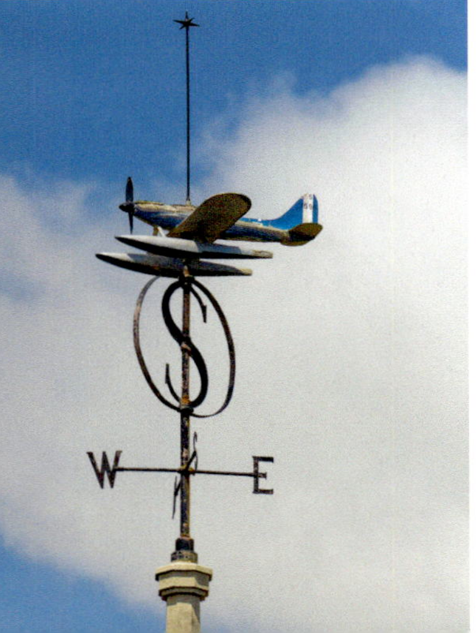

The weathervane in Greenhill Gardens marks the exploits of George Hedley Stainforth.

X Buses

If you want to view all the glories Weymouth and the adjoining Jurassic Coast has to offer and do not want to have your attention taken away from the stunning views by driving, you want the number X 53 bus.

The X 53 will pick you up from Weymouth railway station or by the statue of King George on the Esplanade and convey you along the scenic B3157 road through the villages that border the landward side of the Fleet Lagoon and on to the other end of Chesil beach at West Bay. Beyond that (and outside the scope of this book) it will take you to the fossil-hunting paradise of Lyme Regis and on to Axminster.

For the ultimate sight-seeing experience check out the X 52 Jurassic Coaster that covers an area much larger than this book but has the advantage of being an open-top bus.

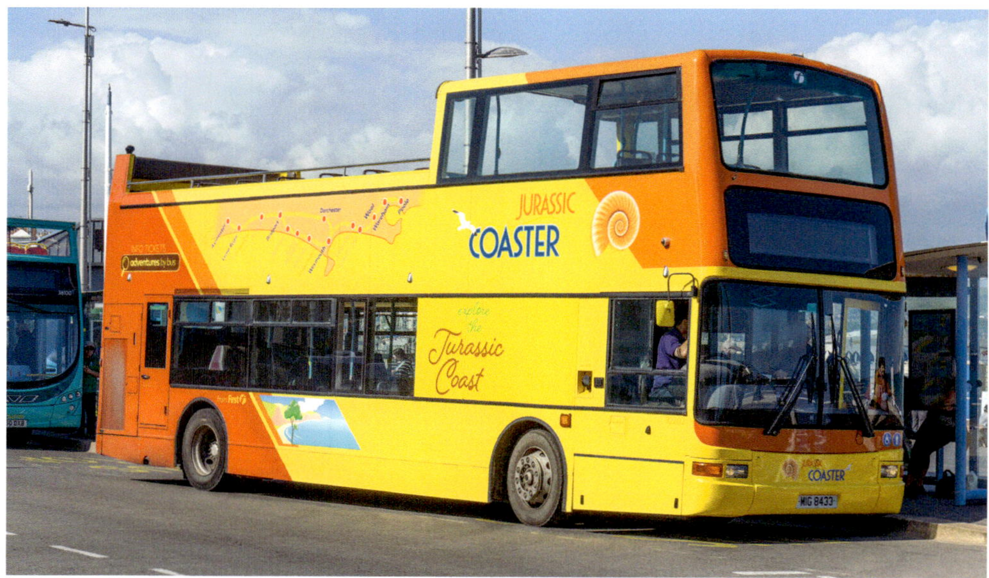

The Jurassic Coaster X route open-top bus.

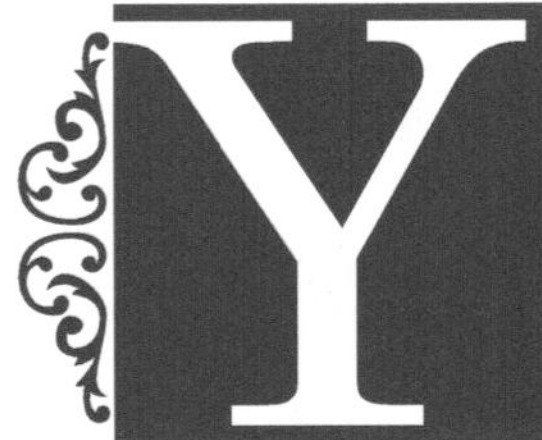

Yachts

On the south side of the harbour on Custom House Quay stands a distinctive building with tall, arched windows in two rows (five above, three on the lower floor) with three blind arched openings above. Sporting the anonymous blue letters 'RDYC', this is the home of the Royal Dorset Yacht Club which offers a 'warm welcome to visiting yachtsmen'.

Previously located on the Esplanade in a building that once housed the Royal Library of King George III, the club moved to their current location in 1975. Prior to their arrival the building has variously been a baths and a 'Seamen's Bethel' where visiting seamen could attend religious services. It was awarded listed status in June 1974.

Founded in January 1875 by ten men at the Kings Arms public house in Dorchester, their club was awarded the admiralty warrant that permitted them to add the prefix 'Royal' to their title and to fly a blue Ensign on their vessels, on 19 of April 1875. A plaque by the door of this welcoming establishment advises visitors that it is also home to the local branch of the Submariners Association once a month.

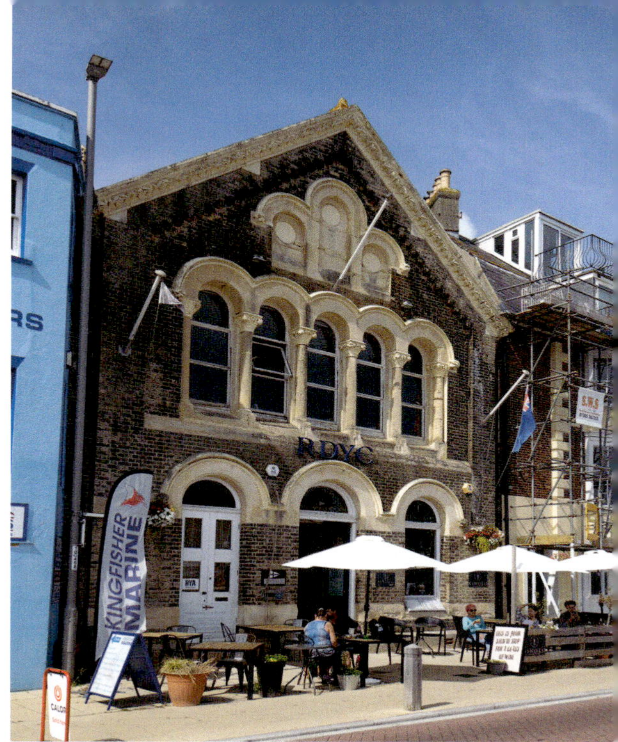

The Royal Dorset Yacht Club on Weymouth Quay.

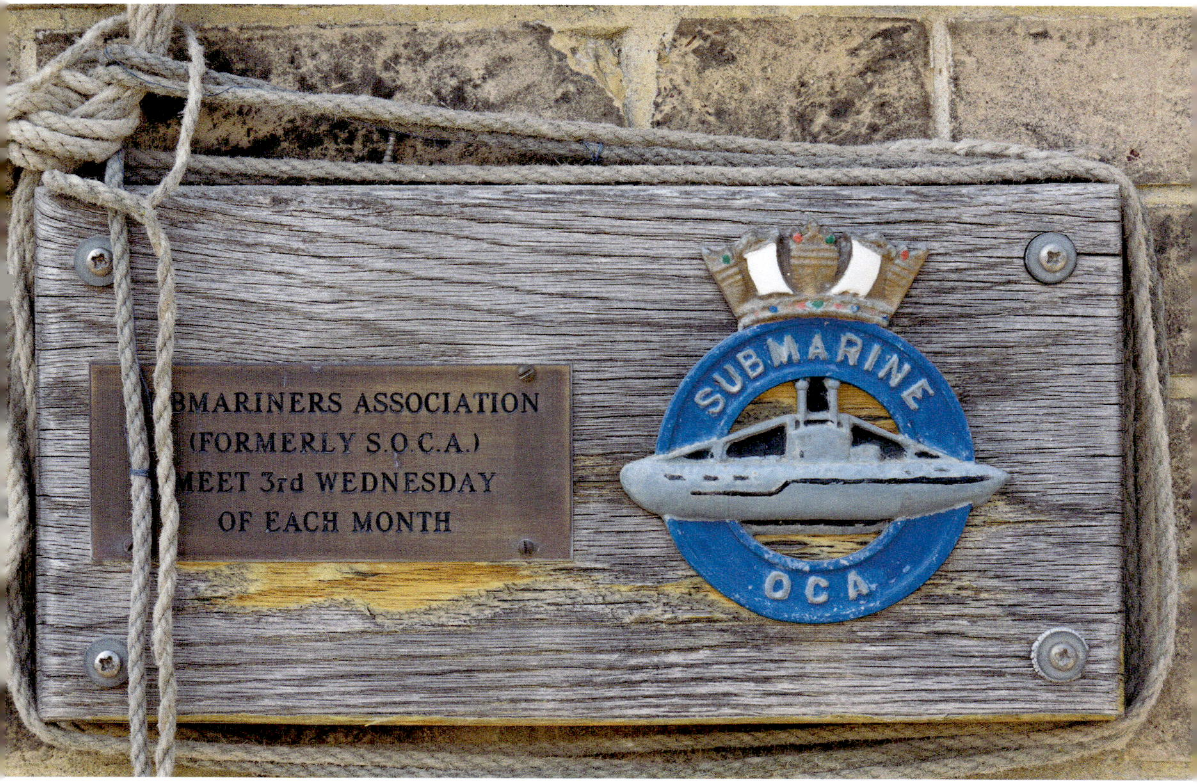

The Royal Dorset Yacht Club also welcomes submariners into their establishment.

Zostera

Also known as eel grass, two types of zostera grow widely submerged in the Fleet Lagoon. During the seasonal die-off in autumn of every year it can be seen washed up on the beaches that border the Fleet Lagoon.